Published by Ravan Press (Pty) Ltd.
P.O. Box 31134
Braamfontein
2017
South Africa
© Copyright Luli Callinicos 1981, 1982, 1985
© Copyright on all photographs and poetry
   used is held by the individual poets and
   photographers
© Copyright on all cartoons: Andy Mason
Cover Design: Carl Becker
ISBN 0 86975 1119 0
Printed by National Book Printers, Goodwood, Cape

First Impression: 1981
Second Impression: 1982
Third Impression: 1985
Fourth Impression: 1989

Acknowledgements

All knowledge is collectively produced, and this book is no exception.

I am especially grateful to the research officers of the Institute of African Studies at the University of the Witwatersrand, to reading groups in Johannesburg and Cape Town, and to Phil Bonner, Doug Hindson, Charles van Onselen, David Webster and Eddie Webster for their useful comments on the manuscript.

This book grew out of the first Social History Workshop held at the University of the Witwatersrand in 1978. I based much of my work on the papers presented there. The Workshop also gave me financial assistance. It is therefore appropriate that the publication of this first volume of *A People's History of South Africa* should coincide with their second workshop.

I would also like to thank Mike Kirkwood, Andy Mason, Dorothy Wheeler, Mpikayipheli Figlan, Rose Zwi and Sandy Parker, of Ravan Press, as well as Janet Callinicos, Carohne Cornell, Lesley Lawson, Kevin Humphrey and Paul Weinberg, for the work they put into the editing and production of this book.

Luli Callinicos
Johannesburg, December 1980

A People's History of South Africa

'Tipping Rock into Ore Box, Crown Mines.'

Volume One:

GOLD AND WORKERS

by Luli Callinicos

Ravan Press   Johannesburg

To
my mother and father
who taught me that knowledge is power
and to
*those who have the capacity to make **this** knowledge powerful.*

Contents

Part Three
Workers' Resistance

QUESTIONS OF A WORKER READING HISTORY

Who built seven-gated Thebes?
Books list the names of kings.
Did kings haul the blocks and bricks?
And Babylon, destroyed so many times
Who built her up so many times? Where
Are the houses where the construction-workers
Of golden-gleaming Lima lived?
Where did the masons go at nightfall
When they finished mortaring the Wall of China?
High Rome is full of victory arches.
Who put them up? Whom did the Caesars
triumph over?

Did chronicled Byzantium build only palaces
for its inhabitants? In fabulous Atlantis
the drowned bellowed in the night when the sea
swallowed them up after their slaves.

Young Alexander conquered India
Just he?
Caesar beat the Gauls.
Didn't he at least have a cook with him?
Philip of Spain wept when his Armada
Went down. Did no one else?
Frederick the Great won out in the Seven Years War.

Who won besides?

A victory on every page.
Who cooked the victory feast?
A great man every decade.
Who paid the bills?

Lots of facts.

Lots of questions.

Bertolt Brecht

Introduction

In less than 20 years, Johannesburg was transformed from bare veld into a rich mining city. In this time black South Africans — neither rich nor citizens — came to work on the mines — and in eGoli.
These men and women were the forerunners of the people who, under today's apartheid system, continue to produce South Africa's wealth.

They live in townships and hostels around Johannesburg and the other industrial cities which have since developed. *Their* history has still to be written.

This volume is the first in a series. It is simply written, yet history is never simple. It tries to analyse the basic issues. It is offered as one contribution to the work that still has to be done.

It studies the rise of the gold mining industry from 1886 to 1924. Why? We believe that gold mining laid down a pattern. It became the pattern of a special form of capitalism. This developed in South Africa over the years and continues to develop. Our history tries to understand its origins.

There are different ways to tell every story, and the same is true of history. For instance, the story of the gold mining industry has often been told as the story of 'progress' — of modernisation, technological achievements, an expanding economy. And 'progress' is most often related as the story of the 'randlords', men like Cecil John Rhodes and Barney Barnato. Told that way, the story shows how they were able to gain fabulous wealth — and, at

the same time, shape the future of a country.

The same story can be told a different way, as in this book. We tell it as the struggle for survival of those whose hands made the wealth, the workers who came to eGoli.

Some of these workers were white, and this is their story, too. The great majority were black. When gold production began, their lives were drawn into a system. The system developed until it affected every part of their lives, from the cradle to the grave.

In studying the rise of gold mining we shall also be studying:

(1) **The coming of gold.** The revolutionary changes that the gold mines imposed on South Africa.

(2) **The workers: their creation and control.** The ways in which men and women were forced to leave their land and become wage-earners; how mine-owners and government used their powers to set up: the migrant labour system; the compound system; the contract system; the pass system; and other methods used to control workers and keep

their wages low.

(3) **Workers' resistance.** Workers did not just sit back and accept their situation. There were many ways in which they resisted — desertions, strikes, boycotts, wage campaigns, the beginnings of political action. They struggled over a long period to gain control over their lives and their work. Today, that struggle continues.

This book shows, too, how methods of control on the mines created and used a racial system. This divided workers into a small group of well-paid, privileged, white workers and a massive force of low-paid, black workers.

The system of control is experienced, painfully, by black workers in South Africa every day.

But to experience is not always to know. We need to understand how the system came into being. We need to know how workers long ago experienced it. To do this we need to look at life in South Africa before the coming of gold. And so we begin with a chapter which deals with society in South Africa before industrial times.

PART ONE

THE COMING OF GOLD

The coming of gold brought the industrial revolution to South Africa. In a short space of time, South Africa was transformed from a land economy — in which people lived and worked on the land — to an industrial, capitalist society.

Part I of this book explains how the *nature* and the *needs* of gold mining in South Africa created the conditions for these changes.

Chapter One

South Africa before Industrial Times

South Africa today is an industrial society. People need money to buy most of their daily needs, and the things they buy are manufactured in factories.

We no longer grow our own food, or make our own clothes from home-made materials, or build our own houses. Nowadays, most people work for a wage.

Until about 200 years ago, however, most people in South Africa had no money. For food, they grew crops and kept cattle, sheep and goats. Nearly everything they needed they had to make themselves.

Few people lived in the towns. Most people, white trekkers as well as blacks, lived on the land. From the land, they were able to produce their basic needs. For the sake of convenience, we will call these pre-industrial people *subsistence farmers*, living in a *subsistence society*.

Subsistence society in South Africa was much the same as subsistence societies anywhere in the world: people aimed to reproduce themselves and to feed their families. The most important things therefore were:
- land;
- domestic animals such as

sheep, cattle or goats;
- the family and family labour;
- the community;
- trade.

THE IMPORTANCE OF LAND

Land was vital in subsistence society for many reasons. Land provided people with crops for food; it supported cattle and other animals which were used for food, clothing and labour. Land also provided the materials such as clay, bricks and thatch for building houses.

Without the right to use land, people in subsistence society could not survive. Many wars were fought over the ownership or use of land.

The quality of land was very important, too. Land with rivers, or land with good pasture was in

great demand. The Tswana, for example, settled near springs; the main chiefdoms in Zululand developed in areas where there was the best combination of soil, pasturage and water. This access to good land was a great help in building up their cattle, wealth and power in later years.

CATTLE

In South Africa cattle were very important for both black and white subsistence farmers. Cattle provided milk and meat; their skins were used for clothes and shoes.

In black societies, cattle were used for religious ceremonies and also for lobola, which was an important part of the economy. Lobola was an exchange of cattle for a fruitful marriage. If the

2

Left: Women were all trained in pottery, but the work of the best potters was always in demand.

Below: Craftsmen forged iron into farming tools and weapons of hunting and war. Iron workers held an honoured position in society.

wife proved infertile, her family would be obliged to give in marriage a second daughter. Lobola also enabled the bride's brothers in turn to afford the lobola for marriage and children themselves. Lobola circulated wealth and helped to build up the population and labour power of the family.

A man's wealth and power were therefore measured by his cattle.

THE FAMILY

Because of people's close ties to the land in subsistence society, it was important to have enough labour to work it. More labour produced more food. This labour came from the family. Families in subsistence societies were large — they usually consisted of the father, his wives and children, plus any unmarried relatives who might be needing a home.

The members of the family worked together to produce their basic needs. They shared many of the daily tasks. At the same time, each member of the family had his or her own job. The women would usually grow the food and prepare it. They were skilled in pottery and made other things for the home. They also raised the children. The older girls helped the adult women in their tasks.

The men hunted and supervised the older boys, training them to look after the animals. In time, a man became the head of a family, with a duty to protect it in times of danger.

Some men were trained to do specialist tasks — there were

people who were healers and spiritual leaders, some were musicians, others learned the craft of iron-making. Iron-makers held an honoured position in subsistence society. They had a valuable skill, providing farmers with iron implements and soldiers with weapons of war.

It is easy to see why people wanted large families in subsistence societies — more people would make work easier to share out. Even children played their part in helping the family to survive, doing whatever small tasks they could. Children were always welcome in subsistence societies.

THE COMMUNITY

The family was able to make or produce most of what it needed. But there were some tasks that could not be performed by the family alone. Hunting, for example, needed to be carried

out by a large party of men, more than a family could provide.

Sometimes, too, there were dangers. People needed to protect themselves. Large groups or communities gave them strength against natural hazards, and against those who tried to take their land away from them.

As the groups grew larger, they developed into *chiefdoms*. The leader or chief was expected to speak and act on behalf of the community.

Loyalty to the community was very important in subsistence society, for the community worked for the well-being of all its members. The community would not hesitate to make sacrifices to help if one of its kinsfolk was in trouble. Life-long friendships were formed by members of the same age-group, and hospitality, too, was most important.

In subsistence society, there-

3

fore, people were *community based* — they did not think of working only for themselves, or for their immediate family alone, but saw themselves as members of a community. Their fortunes rose or fell with the fortunes of the community.

In African subsistence societies in particular, there were no great class differences. This was mainly because there were no great property owners. No one man could have land to own and use as he liked. He could use the land, but if he used it badly, then the chief would take it back.

The chief decided how much land each family needed, so that there would be no disputes.

In South Africa, most black subsistence farmers were skilled farmers working under difficult conditions. Although land was plentiful a few hundred years ago, there was not much rainfall and the soil was not rich. But farmers practised methods of soil conservation and irrigation. They were quick to improve farming methods and to cultivate new crops such as mealies and tomatoes, which were brought from outside Africa.

When the land no longer produced good crops or good grazing for the animals, people moved on to new land together, while the old land rested.

In later years, when whites came to South Africa, they, too, moved in groups, and they, too, appointed leaders to be their chiefs to prevent quarrelling and to organise fighting in times of war.

TRADE

Although the community was mostly able to produce its own needs, there nevertheless was some brisk trading in subsistence society. In hard times, such as drought, trade helped to get essential food for the community. In good times, when the community produced more than it needed, they used their surplus to trade for additional goods which they could not easily produce themselves.

In the wetter climate of Zululand, for example, it was easier to grow good crops of maize. The people there were able to exchange this maize for oxen, which were bred in the drier uplands. Hundreds of years ago, the Venda and the Phalaborwa were using their access to iron to conduct regular trading from the western Transvaal (as we know it today) right across to the coast.

Trade was also conducted with non-Africans. Ivory, iron, tin and animal skins were much sought

The trading post.

after by Arab and European trading ships many years before white settlement in South Africa. Blacks would exchange these goods for glass beads, brass and, later, guns.

Up to about 200 years ago, however, trade was not so important as to change the nature of subsistence society. The basic things used by people continued to be made or produced by the family itself. Very few people depended completely on trade for a living.

Then, gradually, things began to change.

HOW LAND BECAME SCARCE

As long as there was enough land, black subsistence farmers could survive. But slowly land became scarce.

More and more people were filling up the land; the population was growing. Sometimes, when chiefdoms moved to new land, they found other people there already.

The result was a great land hunger. People began to fight for more land. Battles over land became more and more frequent and severe. Eventually wars began to change the traditional, subsistence way of life.

The communities became more organised. The successful chiefdoms grew in size, taking over smaller chiefdoms. They began to support growing armies of young men with food and specially made weapons.

The chief became more power-

The search for land became more desperate when Dutch and British settlers trekked inland.

ful. He had greater control over what the community produced. He also controlled the spoils of war — cattle and other animals captured from the losers. The system of government changed, too. Where there had been traditional systems of consultation, these often disappeared. The chief took on the powers of a king, and a privileged class of hand-picked 'indunas' emerged — an aristocracy with more power and more wealth than the counsellors of old.

THE MFECANE

About 200 years ago, the land shortage came to a head. There followed a period of great upheaval in black subsistence soci-

ety. The land wars started a chain reaction throughout South Africa, scattering people as far as central and East Africa.

New groupings and new chiefdoms came into being. Thousands were killed in the wars, thousands more fled from their traditional pastures, taking refuge in caves or in the mountains. Thousands more were captured and absorbed by the conquering chiefdoms. Other wandering refugees banded together to form new communities for their own protection. It was during this time that nations like the Zulu, Basotho and Ndebele came into being.

This period became known as the *Mfecane* (the crushing) or the *Difaqane* (forced migration).

WHITE COLONIALISM

In the midst of the upheaval of the Mfecane, Dutch settlers entered the scene. They had arrived in the Cape in 1652 and set up a colony there. They had destroyed subsistence life by taking the land from the Khoi and the San (whom they called 'Hottentots' and 'Bushmen'). To farm the land, they used the Khoi — as well as slave labour, mostly from Malaya. A hundred and fifty years later, British colonists arrived to take over the Cape. Many of the Dutch settlers were unhappy with British rule and proceeded to move into the interior, looking for new land.

The white trekkers only dimly understood what was happening to black society. They, too, were subsistence farmers in search of new land. Nevertheless, they profited from the Mfecane. Large areas were deserted. When black farmers came from their places of refuge after the wars to their traditional pastures, white settlers had already claimed them.

There began a bitter struggle for land, first in the eastern Cape between the Xhosa and the Dutch and later the British, then in Natal between the Zulus and the Dutch and the British, and then in the interior.

HOW BLACKS LOST THE STRUGGLE FOR LAND

For a large part of the 19th century, blacks and whites were in a deadlock. In the Soutpansberg in the Transvaal, the Venda were actually pushing the white trekkers back from their frontiers. In the eastern Cape and in Zululand, land wars dragged on until the 1870s.

The turning point came when Britain sent large armies to South Africa. They settled the outcome. With their horses, their modern guns and their cannons, they were eventually able to crush the Xhosa in the eastern Cape and the Zulus in Natal (but only after the British lost over 1 000 men in just one battle at Isandhlwana in 1879).

By this time, fighting had become as important as farming. Young men were spending more and more time at war, and less time with the cattle and the land.

As black farmers began to lose the struggle for land, it became clear that there was no longer enough land for most people to live a subsistence life.

The land that was left could not support all the subsistence farmers. Some of them began to work for the white farmers in return for the right to farm a piece of land, and perhaps some food or a calf as payment each year.

HOW TRADE GREW

War was not the only form of contact between black and white

A settler farm in the early years of colonialism, using slave labour.

farmers: trade was becoming more and more important. As white settlers spread further into the country they began to exchange cattle and other goods with black farmers.

Traders from Durban and Cape Town began to bring goods like knives, blankets, ploughs and things which subsistence farmers did not easily make — and in this time of war, guns were in great demand.

As time went on, trade became more important. People began to make fewer pots, tools, clothes and other everyday things. They began to rely more on traders' goods.

MONEY

At first they traded by exchange. But as trade became established, traders began to ask for money instead of goods — money was easier to exchange and easier to transport. So black farmers had to find money to buy the traders' goods.

One way they did this was to *sell* their extra crops or wool in the white settler towns. Many began to prosper; and between about 1830 and 1890 there emerged a flourishing African peasantry. (However, their good fortune was not to last — see

Chapter Six.)

Black farmers found they needed money for another reason — to pay taxes.

When the Boers and the British took over the land, they formed governments, which ruled over blacks as well as whites.

These Boer and British governments soon began to demand taxes from the people they ruled. Blacks had to pay a hut tax as well as a poll tax. The poll tax was a tax of one pound — or about two Rand — for every man over 18 years of age. These taxes were collected in money.

As time went on, most subsistence farmers got this money for taxes by going out to work for a short time on white farms or in the towns. They would earn some money as workers and then come back home when they had earned enough to pay the tax man or the trader.

CHANGES

So even before the discovery of diamonds and gold, colonialism had changed subsistence life.
* The first important change came with the shortage of land. Black subsistence society was slowly being destroyed as they lost the struggle for land.
* The second important change came when black subsistence

farmers started to use things which the family or tribe did not make. They bartered these goods with traders.
* The third important change came when black subsistence farmers found they needed money for trade and for tax. Some managed to produce enough extra crops to sell, but most had to leave their land for a time and become workers by selling their labour.

Each of these changes took black subsistence farmers another step away from subsistence society. Each of these changes took them a step closer to the time of the industrial revolution, when thousands of subsistence farmers would be forced to leave home to become workers on the mines.

THE LOSS OF THE LAND: A POET SPEAKS

We pass where life was,
the sun showing the place every morning,
where every reflection of our eyes
is attracted to our ancestors . . .
Why not the body of the land forever,
why not my *rooigrond* living on,
the spirits of our ancestors buried there?
While false beliefs like glue
hold our new homes together . . .

— from *Old Homes* by David Mphusu. (*Staffrider* Vol 1 No 1)

Chapter Two
The Gold Rush

'Gold — an industry which feared neither locusts nor cattle diseases, neither drought nor summer floods.'[1]

One summer's day in 1886, two prospectors discovered gold on a Transvaal farm called Langlaagte. Gold was not new to the Transvaal. Africans had mined gold hundreds of years earlier. More recently, gold had been found in the Eastern Transvaal, but this gold ran out and the small mining towns closed down. The gold find at Langlaagte was different. The gold discovered there ran for miles and miles underground, 'an endless treasure of gold.'[2]

Gold changed the face of the Transvaal. Before 1886, it had been a poor, struggling Boer republic but ten years later, it was the richest gold mining area in the world. As news of the gold find spread throughout South Africa and the rest of the world, men made their way to the Transvaal.

They walked, they rode on horseback, or they came by slow ox-wagon. Ships no longer passed South Africa on their way to Australia or New Zealand. Instead, boat-loads of men arrived at the ports and hurried to catch the next coach to the Transvaal, hoping to find the riches of their dreams.

Wherever people found gold, another little mining camp grew. Langlaagte became part of a big new mining town called Johannesburg, where many other mining camps were set up. Soon Johannesburg became the biggest town in the Transvaal, bigger even than Pretoria, the capital.

Other mining towns sprang up as well. If you look at the map on page 10 you will see that these mining towns form a line along a ridge. This is called the *Witwatersrand* — the *Rand* for short.

As time passed, the tents disappeared and people began to build houses, offices and shops. Builders were very busy. Ox-carts and horses filled the streets with traffic, dust and noise; yet the sound of the stamps crushing rocks in the mines around the town could be heard day and night.

Every week, hundreds of people poured into the 'golden' Rand — all had come to seek their fortune.

Gold mining was not new to the Transvaal — men and women had mined precious and semi-precious metal many centuries before the coming of the white man to southern Africa.

Above: Early prospectors in 1886, near Ferreirastown, which became part of central Johannesburg.
Below: Market Square, twenty years later.

People of the Mining Towns

There were three main groups of people who hoped to make money from the mines:

* The first to come to the mines were the *prospectors*. These were the men who came to look for gold in the soil. They came with great hopes of 'striking it rich'.

* A growing group of people were *labourers*. Many of them were black farmers needing money. They hoped to find jobs so that they could pay their taxes, or buy guns or tools like hoes and ploughs for their land.

So at first, most labourers did not come to stay. They went home as soon as they had earned enough.

* Other people did not get their money directly from the mines — they made money from the needs of the people who mined the gold. The sellers of land, lawyers, traders, shop-keepers, ox-wagon drivers and many more made their money in this way.

Many traders did well in those early years on the mines. Goods were in short supply; they could charge high prices.

Ox-wagon drivers were also busy. They brought food and water from the farms for the new townspeople. They carried supplies like building materials and machinery from the faraway ports on the coast.

For the first time in South Africa, towns grew so fast that they could not supply people with all their needs. Water was so scarce that people had to buy it by the bottle. Cabbages cost R2 each.

Improved Transport

More and more people were coming to live on the Witwatersrand. As the Rand grew, the seaports became much busier. More and more factory-made goods and machines were being shipped from England to meet the demand.

Goods had to be transported all the way from the coast to the Rand by ox-wagon — and ox-wagons were very slow. Goods were in short supply: the demand was great. Traders saw their chance to make money. No wonder prices were high! But most important, the equipment needed for the mines was taking too long to arrive.

Something had to be done to improve the system of transport. First, the governments of the Transvaal, the Cape and Natal improved the roads so that wagons could travel faster. Then railways were built.

An ox-wagon crossing a drift. Transport was slow and difficult before the coming of the railways.

(Above) Park Station, Johannesburg — 1903.
(Below) Cape Town harbour in the early days. The dockyards developed as trade from the Rand increased.

A map of South Africa, showing the first railway lines to Johannesburg.

You will notice on the map that the first railway lines joined the ports to the mining towns. Most of the main lines went to the Witwatersrand, to the gold mines. (There was also a main line to the diamond mines of Kimberley, in the Cape.)

The coming of the trains to South Africa made a great difference to people all over the country. People living in the countryside used the railways that were built between the towns.
* Men who wanted to work in the gold mines went by train. This made it easier for the mines to get workers.

* Farmers who wanted to sell their crops could send them by train to the larger towns. This meant the towns could get fresh food more easily and cheaply. New stations were built near the bigger white farms to transport the farm produce.
* New towns grew up around the stations. These farming towns gave more work to builders and railway workers, railway officials and traders.

So with the help of the railway lines, more and more towns were built in the interior, providing an increasing number of jobs for the people of South Africa.

A New Way of Life

Industrialisation was spreading from the Witwatersrand to the rest of South Africa. As the Witwatersrand grew, so did the need for goods, machinery, food and — most important of all — people to service and develop these mining towns.

Some people became rich. Others lost everything they had. But for all the people who went to live in the towns, whether they were rich mine-owners, or traders, or poor labourers, money became very important.

Townspeople could not live without money. Even farmers, black as well as white, started to grow crops to sell.

For most people, the old way of life was gone forever. From now on, more and more people would:
- work for a wage;
- buy their food and clothes from a shop;
- live in a compound, a township or a suburb.

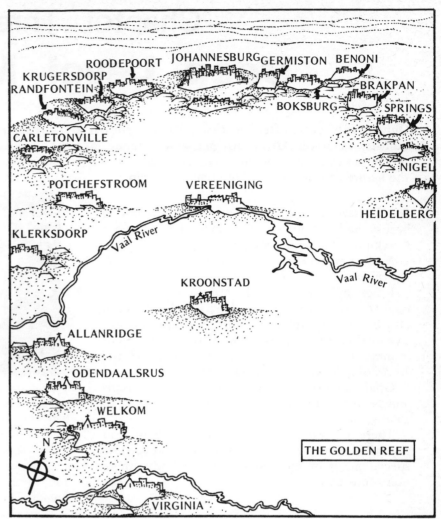

The gold mining towns formed a curve, starting from the east Rand in Heidelberg, extending westwards across to Krugersdorp and Randfontein. Later, gold was discovered further south.

Chapter Three
Deep Level Mining

Only twenty years after the first mine was started at Langlaagte, gold had become the most important industry in South Africa, bringing much money into the country. Gold mining on the Rand created a revolution in mining methods, and changed South Africa in a very significant way. This chapter examines the nature and the needs of the Rand gold mines.

People have always treasured gold for its lasting beauty and usefulness. Thousands of years ago a Greek poet, Sappho, wrote about gold:

Neither rust nor worms can spoil this metal. It has the power to excite the minds of men.

Kings and traders sought after gold because it could be stored for years yet keep its value. It could also be divided into small units and used as coins. Eventually, gold coins became the standard form of money. Later, paper money was used, and the stores of gold were held by governments.

Gold therefore is important for many reasons and people will go to great trouble and expense to find it.

There are four points to remember about gold mining in South Africa which help to explain the special needs of the mines. Let's deal with these points one by one:

(1) Fixed Price

Gold is like all other useful things that are bought and sold. It is the product of human labour. The more labour needed to produce gold, the more valuable it becomes. Governments can fix the price for a time. But as gold becomes more and more difficult to produce, the price eventually has to increase.

When gold was discovered on the Rand the price of gold was fixed and stayed that way for many years. This meant that the mine-owners could not charge more for the gold. To make profits, they had to cut the cost of *producing* the gold. We shall see later how they did this by forcing down the wages of the unskilled workers.

(2) Deep-Level Mining

The right hand photograph illustrates an early outcrop mine. In the picture, labourers are digging with picks and shovels. The gold seems to be near the surface of the ground.

In those days, gold was not difficult to mine — especially if the prospector had many labourers to dig for him!

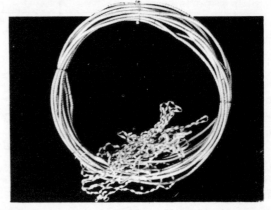

This finely wrought gold necklace is one of many gold artifacts discovered on the hill of Mapungubwe, in the northern Transvaal. It is estimated to be about 800 years old. (Photo, W. Saunderson-Meyer)

But soon, miners found that they had to dig deeper and deeper to find the gold — 100 metres, 500 metres, a kilometre underground and even deeper. This type of mining became known as *deep-level mining.*

Prospectors found that they needed special machines to get the gold that was so deep down — they needed ventilation to provide air and some-

An early outcrop mine.

times, when there was water underground, they needed pumps.

They also realised that the stopes were dangerous. Special props had to be made to stop the stopes from caving in.

There were many problems, and they became

Above: Miners waiting to be lowered down the shaft.
Left: The truck, filled with ore, makes its way three or four metres up the shaft.

Above: The shaft-head and offices of a mine.
Right: This photograph shows how the stope follows the line of gold deposits.

Deep-level mining also needed a massive labour force – and with the price of gold fixed, it had to be cheap.

worse as gold mining went deeper and deeper underground. We shall see later how the problems of deep-level mining were solved.

(2) Low Grade Ore

Page 14 shows how much ore needed to be dug up and crushed to get a very little gold. The reef of gold that runs underground is very thin. It has been compared to a page in a very thick book of rock. In South Africa, there is much less gold in each ton of ore than in other countries that mine gold.

The ore in South Africa, therefore, is poor in gold. It is known as *low-grade ore*.

(4) 'An Endless Treasure of Gold'

At the same time, South Africa is very rich in gold, for the thin reef of gold so deep down under the Witwatersrand stretches for more than 300 miles. The reef stretches from Heidelberg in the east all the way across to Virginia.

This area produces most of the world's gold – and people could carry on mining for hundreds of years.

13

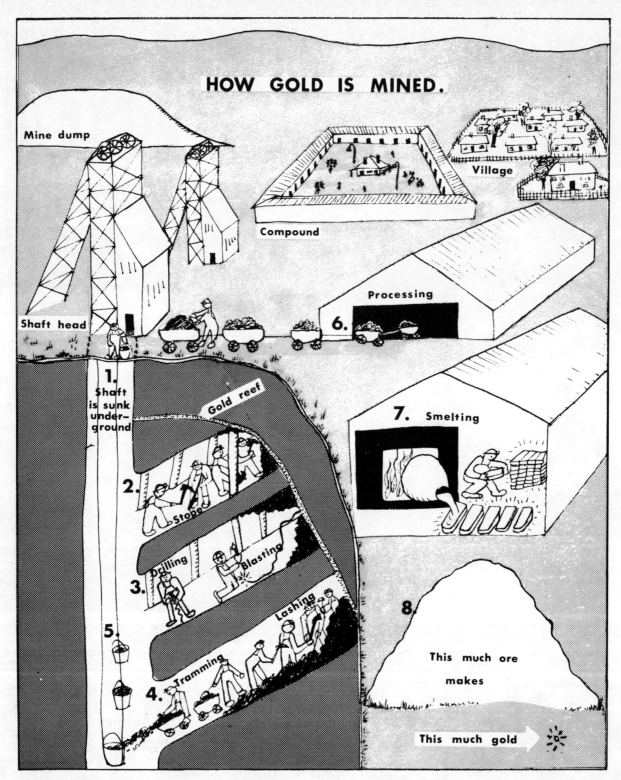

HOW GOLD IS MINED.

Mine dump

Shaft head

Compound

Village

Processing

6.

7. Smelting

1. Shaft is sunk under—ground

Gold reef

2. Stope

3. Drilling Blasting

5.

Lashing

4. Tramming

8. This much ore makes

This much gold →

It is important to understand how gold is mined in South Africa, because the needs of gold mining changed South Africa in a very significant way.

How then, is gold mined?

1. First, at least two shafts are sunk by machines. These shafts go three or four hundred metres underground.

2. Then passages or *stopes* are excavated, leading off from the shaft. The stopes cut across the thin strips of gold or *reefs* that run deeper and deeper underground.

3. Miners find the ore that contains the tiny particles of gold — so tiny that they are invisible to the naked eye. Miners drill holes in the rock around the ore before blasting a small tunnel into the rock.

4. The tunnel has to be cleared of the blasted rock. Men dig the pieces of ore and rock (this job is is called *lashing*) and then load them into trucks (this job is called *tramming*).

5. The ore and rock are taken up to the surface in buckets (called 'skips').

6. The ore is loaded into trucks and taken to another part of the mine works. There, as much gold as possible is separated from the crushed ore. Machines and chemicals are used in this process.

7. There is still some gold left in the ore so the gold is melted. The hot, liquid gold runs out into trays.

8. To make approximately 21 grams of gold, the miners must blast and chop out two tons of ore.

What the Gold Mines Needed

There were three things that created problems for the mine-owners: (1) deep-level mining; (2) low grade ore; and (3) the many miles of gold.

What did they need to overcome their problems?

First of all, deep-level mining of low-grade ore was very expensive, dangerous and difficult. But mine-owners knew that they could make big profits if they produced enough gold and managed to keep down their mining costs, so they were ready to spend millions of rand to start even a low-grade ore gold mine.

* So the first need for the gold mines was lots of money — better known as **capital**.

* The mines needed **special machinery**. As mining went deeper and deeper, more and more expensive machinery was needed. The mine-owners had to import these machines from other countries and pay to transport them to the Witwatersrand.

* The mines had to have **skilled labour**. Experienced men were needed to sink shafts, fit pipes and pumps, instal lifts, build props, drive engines and operate drilling machines — as well as sort and extract the gold from the ore above ground.

At first, there were very few men in South Africa who had experience of deep-level mining. The mine-owners had to get skilled miners from the mines of America and Australia, and from the deep coal mines of Britain. These skilled men demanded high wages for their work.

* The mine-owners also needed thousands of **unskilled labourers.** These workers were needed to do the heavy task of lashing and tramming, and also to hammer small tunnels into the ore.

As' the mines expanded, the

* Each mine also needed **supervisors** to direct and control the thousands of workers. And to keep production working smoothly, the mines needed **managers**.

As the numbers of black unskilled labourers grew, supervisors and managers became more and more important, and, they were paid well. Managers' were the most privileged of all, some of them earning enormous salaries plus many other extras such as free housing and domestic servants.

mine-owners called for more and more labour. Within a few years, many thousands of men were leaving their homes on the land and going to work for wages on the mines. Unskilled workers were paid a very low wage.

Deep-level mining demanded a great deal — huge amounts of capital, knowledge of machinery, careful planning and an organisation of thousands of men — skilled workers, labourers and supervisors. To get their hands on all they needed, the mine-owners had to have great power. Who were these mine-owners and how did they achieve this power? Chaper 5 will try to answer these questions.

'The rich live like princes, waited on by liveried flunkies, rushing about in their motor cars, entertaining, receiving, squandering money like water, growing richer day by day. What wonder that they care little for the condition of the poorer portion of the city?'[1]

Chapter Four
The Randlords

Deep-level mining changed the whole system of gold mining on the Rand. It made mining very expensive. Today, it costs R60 million to start a gold mine — and that is before the first gram of gold is mined.

People needed huge amounts of money to start mining the gold which they would then sell at a profit. Money used in this way is called *capital*. (See the cartoons on this page for a simple explanation of capital.)

A capitalist need not be a mine-owner. He can use his capital to start factories, shops or other businesses.

But in this chapter we are talking about the early capitalists of those deep-level mines. Who were they and where did they get their capital?

CAPITAL FROM THE DIAMOND MINES

The discovery of diamonds brought a great deal of capital to South Africa. People came from England and Europe with capital to buy land and dig for diamonds. Some people made fortunes from the diamonds that they and their workers mined. The diamonds were sold for high prices in Europe and the money came back to the mine-owners in Kimberley.

As the diamond mines grew bigger and deeper, the richer mine-owners bought out more and more of the smaller mines. Because they had the capital, they could pay experts to work out how to mine diamonds deeper down. They could also afford to buy machinery from Europe. Prospectors who had less capital and know-how could not compete with them.

Fifteen years after the discovery of diamonds, a few capitalists controlled the richest diamond mines in Kimberley. They joined together to form a powerful company, De Beers Consolidated Mines. De Beers controlled diamond mining in Kimberley.

An early surface mine. Deep-level mining required much sophisticated machinery. The small miner could not afford this.

When deep-level mining started on the Witwatersrand, the richest diamond mine-owners moved into gold mining. They brought with them considerable capital and experience of mining. They also brought ideas on how to control mine-workers in order to increase production, as you will see in this chapter.

CAPITAL FROM OTHER COUNTRIES

The Kimberley mine-owners brought a lot of capital to the Rand, but it was not enough to start this new industry of deep-level mining. So they started *mining companies.*

They invited people from other countries, especially Britain, to invest capital in their companies. These people then became *shareholders* in the companies and shared the profits from the mines.

But the richest capitalists, the 'Randlords', made sure that they owned most of the shares in their companies. In that way they never lost control of the gold mines.

A lively scene in the Johannesburg Stock Exchange, where gold mining shares were bought and sold.

The Chamber of Mines, established in 1887.

THE CHAMBER OF MINES

The mine-owners did not only need capital to control the gold mines. They also needed careful organisation. They realised that South Africa must change in important ways if their mines were to be as profitable as they wanted them to be. To bring about these changes, the mine-owners needed a great deal of power.

A large part of this book is concerned with the ways in which the mine-owners gained the power and the profits they wanted. In doing so, they brought about far-reaching, in fact revolutionary changes in South Africa.

In the early years, the companies started many different gold mines.

Some struggled to make a profit because their ore was of poor quality, while other mines were doing very well. Some mines were having problems getting skilled miners; others could not find enough unskilled labour. The mines had different managers, and different management policies. Some mines were able to offer higher wages to unskilled workers, while other mines went short of labour.

It seemed clear to many mine-owners that one system was needed for all the gold mines. The mining companies needed to co-operate with one another in order to get the most from their mines.

In 1887, the big mining companies formed a kind of mine-owners' association called the *Chamber of Mines*. The Chamber of Mines became a powerful organisation serving the mining companies and getting them to agree to common policies on wages, finding workers and how to deal with the government.

In later chapters we shall see many examples of how the Chamber of Mines used its power for the benefit of the gold mines and their owners.

GOVERNMENT SUPPORT

Because the mine-owners controlled the gold mines, they also had power over the different governments of South Africa. (South Africa was divided into four states at the time; the Transvaal, Natal, The Cape and the Orange Free State.) The governments did well out of the gold mines, directly or indirectly, so it paid them to help the mine-owners to increase profits.

The Transvaal government benefited most of all from the gold mines. In 1884, for example, it was a desperately poor state — with only a few cents left in the bank! Five years later it had more than R3 million from the mines in taxes, stamp duties from land and property sales, and mining and trading licences. The Cape and Natal governments more than doubled their income from taxing the ports and charging for transport on the railways. Even the Orange Free State benefited from the mines. Farmers were doing well and the value of their land rose.

The gold mines were vitally important to all the governments. The governments were prepared to help those who controlled the mines — the Randlords.

Some mine-owners held important positions in their governments. They could even change government policies when they wanted to.

One of the most powerful mine-owners, Cecil John Rhodes, used his power to help the mine-owners' interests. His story and picture are on the following page.

President Kruger (with his hand on his chest) poses with government members of the Orange Free State and the Transvaal Republic to mark the opening of the first railway bridge linking the south to the Witwatersrand.

* The Randlords were a small group of powerful mine-owners with experience of the Kimberley diamond mines.
* They were able to gain control of the gold mines with the capital they had gained from diamonds.
* They made themselves and the gold mines even stronger by forming the Chamber of Mines to look after their interests.
* Their control over the gold mines also gave them government support. Some mine-owners such as Cecil John Rhodes even had direct political control.

In later chapters we shall see how the powerful mine-owners and their organisation helped to bring about revolutionary changes in South Africa so that the gold mines could remain profitable.

Cecil Rhodes — Mineowner and Empire Builder

Cecil John Rhodes was one of the earliest of the small group of rich and powerful mine-owners in South Africa.

He first came to South Africa from England in 1871 as a sickly boy of 18. He brought with him three thousand pounds which an aunt had lent him and started to work on his brother's diamond diggings in Kimberley.

Soon he was making one hundred pounds a week and in four years he saved enough money to buy up more diggings in the De Beers mine. Rhodes continued buying up diggings — together with his partner, C.D. Rudd, he was fighting against other rich mine-owners for control of the diamond mines.

By 1887 Rhodes had brought together the richest diamond mine-owners in Kimberley, in the *Consolidated De Beers Company*. The company had capital of nearly two and a half million pounds and controlled the diamond industry in South Africa.

When deep-level mining started on the Rand the directors of De Beers Consolidated were able to use their capital to start *Consolidated Gold Fields of South Africa*. Although it was less prosperous than other companies, the gold mines made huge profits for their owners. Rhodes himself was getting up to £400 000 a year from his share in gold.

But Rhodes was not only rich, he was also politically powerful. When he became the Prime Minister of the Cape in 1890 he helped to change laws in the Cape to benefit the mines and industry.

His Glen Grey Act aimed to push more blacks into leaving their land to become wage-earners on the mines and the railways. The Act also tried to break up traditional, subsistence life by dividing tribal land and allowing single families to own small farms, growing crops to sell.

Rhodes played a significant role in the production of ideas. He was chief or part-owner of The Star *newspaper, the* Cape Argus, *the* Cape Times, The Diamond Fields Advertiser, *the* Midland News *and several influential newspapers in England.*

Rhodes wanted blacks to become industrialised and 'Westernised' as quickly as possible. His policy was 'equal rights for every civilised man south of the Zambezi'. But as more and more blacks got educated and earned wages, Rhodes changed the Cape Law to allow the vote only to those who owned property worth seventy-five pounds a year.

Rhodes did not have direct political power over the Boer republic of the Transvaal, however. He often disagreed with the Transvaal government's policies. He felt he could use his money and his power to overthrow the Boer government and instal in its place a British colonial government supporting mine-owners' interests.

In 1895 Rhodes supported an attack on the Transvaal republic. But it was a failure and Rhodes

Rhodes' home in Rondebosch — one of his five residences.

had to resign as Prime Minister of the Cape. (For more details on the quarrel between the Randlords and the Transvaal government, see page 58 on *The Anglo-Boer War and the Mines.*)

Rhodes also used his wealth to pursue his dream of expanding Britain's empire in Africa.

Botswana became a British colony through the efforts of Rhodes and his British South Africa Company police, accompanied by white settlers. The territory was named Mashonaland.They had hoped to start a 'new Rand' from the ancient gold mines of the Mashona, but the gold had been worked out of the ground long before.

The whites became farmers. When the Matabele and the Mashona rebelled against the coming of the whites to their land, the· British South Africa Company police crushed them. The conquered lands were named Southern and Northern Rhodesia, to honour Rhodes. Today, these are the countries of Zimbabwe and Zambia.

Rhodes died in 1902, a millionaire many times over.

What's in a Name?

There is a long and confused history of names for blacks in South Africa. It reflects the changing attitudes of whites towards blacks. Where do these terms come from?

In the period covered in this book, people spoke of *kaffirs, natives, niggers, boys*. Whites used these terms, but we find blacks referring to themselves as *natives,* too.

In the many centuries when Europeans were trading as equals with traders in Africa, they called these people *Africans.* By the 17th century, when Dutch and English settled in the Cape, they were referring to blacks as *kaffirs* (or caffres), after the Arabic word for *pagan,* or non-Muslim. (Of course, to the Arabs, Europeans were kaffirs too.)

In time, with the coming of the missionaries to Southern Africa and the conversion of many blacks to Christianity, the word *kaffir* took on an insulting meaning. By the beginning of this century, the cultured Englishman had dropped *kaffir* in favour of *native* — meaning one who is born in or belongs to a place. The English employers often spoke of black labourers as *boys* — 'coloured' workers were called 'Cape boys'. This term *boy* seemed to them to justify their treatment of their employees.

'The position of Kaffirs is in many respects analogous to that of the child,' argued the editor of the *South African Mining Journal* in 1892, 'and they require special control and supervision.' No doubt it suited employers to think of themselves as the 'fathers' of black workers paying them low wages but at the same time 'teaching' them the ways of 'civilisation'. (A great part of this book shows how employers controlled their workers on the mines, always finding many reasons to justify their actions.)

The word *native* remained the most popular name for blacks amongst English-speaking whites for a long time — they called themselves *Europeans,* in true colonial style, even when they had never been to Europe. But by the 1960s, when South Africa became a republic, it was beginning to dawn on many whites that the word *native* — or *naturel* — implied that whites did not belong to South Africa. If blacks were *natives,* then whites must be 'foreigners' or, at best, 'settlers'.

The South African government officially adopted the term *Bantu* for blacks. However, as the word 'bantu' means 'people', and as blacks were not consulted on the question, most blacks rejected the term as being absurd and associated with the policy of apartheid.

The more liberal of the English-speaking South Africans at the time began to switch to *Africans.* Afrikaners, of course, could not use the term as they were already calling themselves Africans in

Afrikaans. When blacks were discussed in general, however, they were referred to as non-whites.

In recent years, more and more whites have become aware of the growing power of black consciousness. They are beginning to talk about *blacks* although they often mean by this, Africans only — they continue to refer to 'coloureds' and 'Indians' as well.

Although fashions in names change, in our racial society, the confusion remains.

PART TWO

THE WORKERS
Their Creation and Control

'The plentiful supply of cheap labour made possible the working of the low-grade ore of the Witwatersrand.' Van der Horst, *Native Labour in South Africa*, 1941.

Part I showed how gold mining created a small class of powerful capitalists. It also created a huge working class. Who were these workers? What were the conditions of their work? Part II shows how the mines got their labour and how they kept it cheap.

Chapter Five

How the Mines got their Labour
Taxation

The mines needed labour. Most of all, they needed many thousands of unskilled workers to dig out the ore from underground.

* In 1890, before deep-level mining started, there were 14 000 labourers working on the gold mines.

* By 1899, only five years after deep-level mining started, nearly 100 000 labourers were employed on the Rand mines.

Deep-level mining needed them by their thousands. The more workers each mine had, the more gold could be produced — and the better the profits.

Who were these labourers?

They were black subsistence farmers and peasants who came to the mines to work for wages. They came from all over South Africa and from other countries in Africa. They came to earn money to pay for taxes, farming tools or guns, or because they could no longer support their families on the little land that was left after the coming of the whites.

SHORTAGE OF LABOUR

At first, before deep-level mining started, there were enough black subsistence farmers willing to go to the Witwatersrand for a short while to earn some money. But as the mines got bigger and deeper, the mine-owners began to call for more labour.

'We must have labour,' said the President of the Chamber of Mines. 'The mining industry without labour is as bricks would be without straw, or as it would be to imagine you could get milk without cows.'[1]

But the problem of the mine-owners was that there was no

ready-made working class, no established herd of 'cows'. The mine-owners would have to make one. They would have to find ways of forcing thousands of subsistence farmers and peasants off the land and into the mines.

There were a number of different ways in which the mine-owners managed to do this.

GOVERNMENT HELP

In the last chapter we saw how important the mines were to the government. We also saw how powerful the mine-owners were. When the mine-owners called for

a large supply of cheap labour, the government passed laws to help them.

The government helped them to get labour in two important ways:

(1) They made laws on taxes.

(2) They made laws about land.

In this chapter we shall look at the tax laws.

TAXES

The government used taxes to get people to leave their lands and go to work on the mines. How did they do that?

The government made new

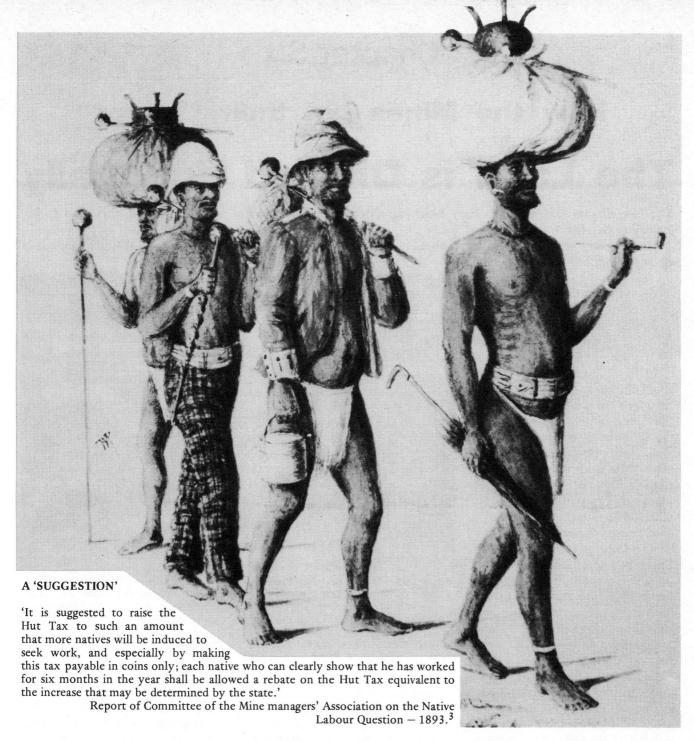

A 'SUGGESTION'

'It is suggested to raise the Hut Tax to such an amount that more natives will be induced to seek work, and especially by making this tax payable in coins only; each native who can clearly show that he has worked for six months in the year shall be allowed a rebate on the Hut Tax equivalent to the increase that may be determined by the state.'

Report of Committee of the Mine managers' Association on the Native Labour Question – 1893.[3]

laws saying that taxes had to be paid with money – not with cattle as before. But subsistence farmers did not have much money. So people had to leave the land and earn money to pay the taxes.

Black subsistence farmers had to pay a number of taxes.

* **There was the hut tax.** The tribes had to pay one Rand for every hut. Eighty years ago a man who worked hard for three months on the mines could earn enough money to pay the hut tax for himself, his family and his parents. So, many subsistence farmers went to work on the mines to earn this money.

* **Black farmers also had to pay a poll tax.** Every man, black or white, who was older than 18 years old had to pay a poll tax of R2 every year. (In the Cape, the poll tax was R4.) Black unskilled workers were earning anything from five cents to 19 cents a day on the mines. Out of that money they had to buy food and clothes for themselves. It took them months of extra work on the mines to pay for the poll tax.

* **Then there was the labour tax.** In the Cape, the prime minister and mine-owner Cecil John Rhodes, passed a law called the Glen Grey Act. This law forced blacks in the Cape to pay R1

every year. But they did not have to pay this tax if they could prove that they worked for wages for three months. In this way, the Cape government tried to push more men into working for wages.

The government aimed to do two things with these taxes:
* Firstly, they aimed to collect money to build roads, railways and offices, and to pay government officials.
* Secondly, they wanted to help the mines. One government report in 1903 openly said that the taxes were specially made to 'force the Natives to work in the towns and on the mines.'[2]

Chapter Six

How the Mines got their Labour

The Land is Divided Unequally

The last chapter showed that many black subsistence farmers became workers because they had to get money to pay taxes.

Many others were forced to leave home and become workers because they had lost so much land. This chapter describes what happened.

By the end of the last century most of the land in South Africa had been taken over by white farmers, by mining companies or by the government.

In the Cape and Natal, land in the Transkei and in Zululand still belonged to black farmers but there was much less than there used to be. The Xhosa and the Zulu lost much of their land after they were defeated on the battlefield. The land in these places was owned by the whole tribe. The chief decided who should use the land.

The Cape government and its Prime Minister, Rhodes, wanted blacks to buy land for themselves (as individuals) and not to share it with other families. They knew that those who failed to buy land would have to go out and work for wages.

Individual land-owners also had to pay extra tax to the government, as well as paying the costs of fencing their land. The result was that very few of them remained full-time subsistence farmers.

Either they lost their land or they began to grow crops to sell to the growing number of people in the mines and the towns. They became peasant farmers, like many Boers.

There were also black commercial farmers in the Orange Free State and the Transvaal. Very little land was still owned by black tribes in these provinces. The black farmers here did not farm their own land. Most of them lived on land that belonged to white farmers or they farmed unused land that belonged to mine-owners or the

A successful black sugar farmer in Groutville, Natal. As the Rand developed, a number of black farmers prospered, selling food to the growing towns. The Land Act, however, effectively put a stop to much of the black commercial farming.

government. These farmers were called *squatters.*

SQUATTERS

There were thousands of squatters in the OFS and the Transvaal. Some were whites, but most were black.

Squatters grew their own crops and gave half to the landowner for part of the year or they paid rent in cash to the landowner. Many of these squatters made money from selling their crops to the towns.

TWO POWERFUL GROUPS

Meanwhile, as the Witwatersrand began to grow, two powerful groups began asking the Transvaal government to make new laws about the land. Both these

groups were important to the government.

* One group was the white commercial farmers, the Boers. They were important to the government because they had voted for it and for President Kruger.

* The other important group was the mine-owners. The Transvaal government wanted to look after them because the mines brought great riches to the Transvaal.

COMMERCIAL FARMERS

The Boers had very large farms — they had taken for themselves most of the land in the Transvaal and the Orange Free State during the Great Trek. But for a long time they were not able to use all this land. Instead, they allowed squatters to use the land in

A commercial farmer with his labourers. As the gold mines and the towns developed, commercial farmers began to require more and more labour.

return for crops and labour.

When many of the Boers became commercial farmers, after the discovery of minerals, they needed more labour. They needed more workers to grow crops and rear cattle to sell to the growing mining towns.

In 1895, the same year that the hut tax and the poll tax came into force in the Transvaal, the government passed a *'squatters' law'*. The law aimed to help the Boers to overcome the labour shortage. According to the law, only five black families were allowed to 'squat' on any white man's farm. All other squatters had to leave the land and find work as labourers on other farms, or else on the mines or in the towns.

But the law did not work very well. There were whole tribes living on land that was supposed to belong to white farmers. These people had been living there for many years, since before the Boers trekked to the Transvaal. All over the Transvaal, many families stayed where they were and continued to work part of the time for their Boer land-lords.

As the years went by, white commercial farmers continued to call on the government for more labour. The towns were growing rapidly and needed more food. To produce more food, the commercial farmers needed more land as well as more labour. They

wanted to exploit all their land.

Their eyes turned to the black squatter farmers, who were using 'white' land to grow and sell crops. The white farmers did not approve of this, because they wanted the land that the squatters were using. They also wanted the squatters for labour. But as long as the squatters could use land for themselves, they were unwilling to leave home and work for wages.

THE MINE-OWNERS

The mine-owners also needed cheap labour. They already had many blacks coming to the mines to earn money for taxes. But there was still not enough labour to satisfy the needs of deep-level mining.

The mine-owners knew that most blacks were farmers. They also realised that as long as there was land to support black farmers they would not go to the mines.

Black squatters no longer owned the land, but they were still able to live off it.

'The native has been left, in effect, in undisturbed ownership of the land, and is rapidly becoming the small farmer of the community — able to live, prosper and preserve his independence by the sale of products obtained from the soil,' wrote the editor of the *SA Mining*

Journal in 1895.

'The native . . . cares nothing if industries pine for want of labour when his crops and home-brewed drink are plentiful,' complained the President of the Chamber of Mines in 1912.[1]

The mine-owners saw that the only way to get more black farmers to leave the land was to take it away from them.

So when white farmers began to call for laws against squatters the Chamber of Mines supported them. White commercial farmers and the Chamber of Mines agreed on one thing: **black squatters must get off the land.**

THE LAND ACT

In 1913, the South African government made a law which divided the land between blacks and whites.

The law said that no whites could own land in African areas, and no African could own land in white areas, except in the Cape. If Africans lived on white-owned land, they must work for the landowner. Otherwise, they must live as farmers in the tribal lands, the 'Reserves'.

The map on page 26 shows how the land was divided in 1913. The 'Reserves' formed less than a tenth of the land in South Africa.

WHAT WERE THE RESULTS OF THIS LAW?

1. After the 1913 Land Act, the only land Africans could farm for themselves was the tribal land in the Reserves. But the Reserves were already crowded — there was no room for extra people, so few squatters were able to settle in the Reserves.

2. White commercial farmers got more land to use and more labour. Everybody who lived on their land had to work for them. People who were not needed as workers had to go.

3. The Land Act stopped black farmers from renting land from white farmers.

4. The mines got more labour because the Land Act forced many squatters into the towns to look for work. The easiest way to get a job was in the mines, because the mines were always short of labour.

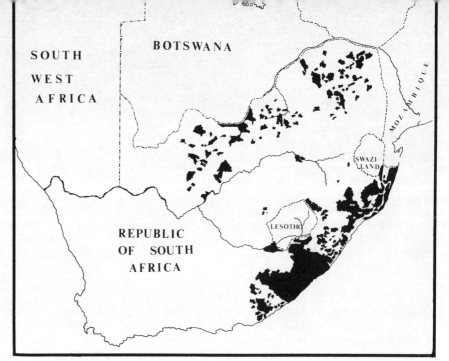

The 1913 Land Act reserved less than 10% of the land for black ownership.

So the Land Act pushed thousands of squatter farmers into becoming wage workers. The government helped the mines to get labour in two ways: through making laws on taxes and through the Land Act, which deprived black farmers of most of their means of production by dividing the land unequally between Africans and whites.

Sol Plaatje — black novelist, poet, journalist and leading political figure — described the sufferings of squatters after the Land Act:

A month after the Land Act was made law, Plaatje and some friends rode on their bicycles around the farms of the Transvaal and the OFS. They wanted to see for themselves what was happening to the squatters. Plaatje wrote many stories about what he saw. He put all these stories into a book called *Native Life in South Africa*. This book was published in 1916 three years after the Land Act.[2]

Here is one of the stories told to Plaatje by a squatter family after the Land Act.

A Black Writer looks at the 1913 Land Act

A squatter called Kgobadi got a message from his father-in-law in the Transvaal. His father-in-law asked Kgobadi to try to find a place for him to rent in the Orange 'Free' State.

But Kgobadi got this message only when he and his family were on their way to the Transvaal. Kgobadi was going to ask his father-in-law for a home for the family. Kgobadi had also been forced off the land by the Land Act.

The 'Baas' said that Kgobadi, his wife and his oxen had to work for R36 a year. Before the Land Act, Kgobadi had been making R200 a year selling crops. He told the 'Baas' he did not want to work for such low wages. The 'Baas' told Kgobadi to go.

So both Kgobadi and his father-in-law had nowhere to go. They were wandering around on the roads in the cold winter with everything they owned. Kgobadi's goats gave birth. One by one they died in the cold and were left by the roadside for the jackals and vultures to eat.

Mrs Kgobadi's child was sick. She had to put her child in the ox-wagon which bumped along the road. Two days later, the child died.

Where could they bury the child? They had no rights to bury it on any land. Late that night, the poor young mother and father had to dig a grave when no one could see them. They had to bury their child in a stolen grave.

Plaatje ended the story with the bitter words that even criminals who are hanged have the right to a proper grave. But under the cruel workings of the Land Act, little children, 'whose only crime is that God did not make them white', sometimes have no right to be buried in the country of their ancestors.

Chapter Seven
The Migrant Labour System

This chapter discusses how the mines used migrant workers to provide cheap labour. 'Migrant' workers were those who left their homes in various parts of southern Africa and travelled long distances to the mines. They worked for a certain time, then they went home again. This system of using migrant workers on a mine (or a farm or a factory) is called the *migrant labour system*.

The Migrant Workers

When the gold mines started, migrant labour was not new. In South Africa there were many migrant workers before the discovery of diamonds and gold. In the summer time, farm labourers used to travel from their homes to the white farms to work there. They would go home again when the season was over. In Natal, many Indians were brought from India to work on the sugar farms for five or ten years. Some went home again. Others stayed in South Africa.

When diamond and gold mining started, thousands of men became migrant workers. Most of them were black farmers. They left their land for a while to work for wages in the mines.

At first, only the young, unmarried men left. They were sent by their chiefs who needed their wages to pay taxes. These taxes had been imposed on the people by the government. A few young men left of their own accord.

As time went by, people needed more and more money. Married men, too, became migrant workers. They were forced to earn money for their families — just as, before this, the young single men had worked to earn money for the chiefdom. The identity of the chiefdom was breaking down. Soon the family unit was also threatened. The time the men spent away from home became longer. It took them longer to earn the money that their families needed.

Each time they went back to work, they would hope it was for the last time. They hoped that *this* time they would save enough money to support the family so that they could stay at home and go back to farming.

But most men remained migrants until they were too old to work for themselves again.

Another Blanket

Mohokare, now I put on another blanket,
Now that I have crossed you,
Wash me from the touch I have had
With woman at home.
Here I cross to the other side.
And I do not know what dangers face me.
Perhaps this is the last time I cross you here.
And if ever I have the chance of crossing you again
Wash me clean, Mohokare, and make me a pure
                                                            man
Make me a man who is fit to go to heaven
Cleanse me from my sins because I am going to
The dangerous place where I may lose my life.

Now if ever I do not come back it will be just
                                                            unfortunate.
But now that I have crossed you,
All the evil things I have done
May they move with you and go down.

In crossing the river I become a new man,
Different from the one I was at home.
At home I was secure
But now that I am on this side
I am in a place of danger,
Where I may lose my life at any time.
So prepare me for my death.

Now that I am this side
I assume a different attitude from the one
Where they are soft with other men.
This side they have to be tough to assume
                                                            manhood
Not be soft like the women at home.
                    (from *Another Blanket*, published by AIM)

ANOTHER BLANKET

For many years Sotho migrants have sung a song as they crossed the Caledon River (Mohokare) and come to work on the Rand mines. The song expresses their feelings as the journey changed them from farmers to workers:

TWO LIVES

Most migrant workers had two very different lives:
* One life was at home on the land, working with the family and with friends.
* The other life was in the towns or the mines, working with machines and with many strangers, often in a hostile atmosphere.

In one life they were family men, loved and respected as sons, husbands and fathers.

In the other, they lost their dignity and even their humanity. Young or old, black workers were referred to as '*boys*'; one mine-owner called them 'mere muscular machines' — there only to produce wealth for their employers.

Work lost its old meaning. As migrant workers they worked for strangers — they worked for a wage.

One family — two worlds.

WHITE TOWNSPEOPLE BUT BLACK MIGRANTS

Not all migrants were black. There were also white mine-workers on the mines. Many of them came from other countries, others were struggling white farmers looking for jobs. They were all new to the Witwatersrand, and most of them hoped to earn enough money to be able to go home again. Most of them never went back. They sent for their families to join them and became full-time wage-earning workers. They became the townspeople of the Witwatersrand.

But black migrants could not settle with their families in the towns. There were a number of reasons for this:
* Firstly, their wages were too low. Black miners were paid just enough to support a single man in town and not a family. The land in the Reserves had to support the migrant's family.
* Secondly, there were no houses for black miners' families on the mines. The miners themselves slept in compounds.
* Thirdly, the Pass Laws would not allow migrant workers to settle with their families in the towns. (We shall be looking at the Pass Laws in Chapter 10.)

THE MINE-OWNERS AND THE MIGRANT LABOUR SYSTEM

In the early years of mining, the mine-owners did not like the migrant labour system very much. They complained because men would come to work for a short while in the mines and then they would leave. '*The native ... reluctantly offers himself or one of his family as industrial worker for just so long as the hut tax can be earned,*' grumbled a President of the Chamber of Mines.[1] The mine-owners at first preferred black farmers to be cut off from the land completely, so that they could become full-time workers. Rhodes, as prime minister of the Cape as well as a leading mine-owner, passed the Glen Grey Act in 1894 to try to force people off the land. He told his government that the law '*removed Natives from that life of sloth and laziness, taught them the dignity of labour and made them contribute to the prosperity of the state. It made them give some return for our wise and good government.*'[2]

Although this particular law was not too successful, its aim was clear; to provide labour for the mines.

White immigrant workers were able to settle in the towns with their families.

CHEAPER FOR THE MINES

As the years went by, the mine-owners began to see that the migrant labour system suited them very well. It was cheaper to feed and house just one worker instead of paying wages to support a whole family in the towns.

Mine-owners wanted black workers, but they did not want black families. They wanted the families to stay behind in the Reserves. They wanted their black workers to have just enough land in the Reserves for their families to live on. But there must not be enough land to support them fully. 'The surplus of young men must earn their living working for a wage,' they said.[3]

So the black migrant labour system was cheaper for the mines. The Chamber of Mines did not have to worry about building houses for the families of unskilled workers. It did not

Children without fathers.

have to worry about building schools and hospitals for old people, women and children. The people in the Reserves would have to look after themselves. Reserves would support them, with some help from the black miners' wages. **The system of migrant labour saved the mine-owners millions of rands every year.**

In the midst of trouble and sorrow
We left our children at home
Children full of tears,
Crying tears: 'Father is gone, is gone,
God, help fathers to return.'
Happiness is returning with spears.

(Sotho song.)[6]

The 'Reserves' Support the Mines

1893: *'Man for man, blacks are better farmers than the Europeans.'* (Traveller in the Cape.)[4]
1932: *'Actual desert conditions have in fact been created where once good grazing existed.'* (Government report.)[5]

We have seen that black farmers were forced off the land into wage labour. This did not happen because they were bad farmers. In fact, in the early years of the mining towns black farmers in different parts of South Africa produced a surplus of food which they were able to sell to the towns.

Yet we find that the picture had changed forty years later. Black farmers by then were struggling, producing less and less from the land. In this chapter we try to understand what brought about this change. We look at the 'reserves' — the other end of the migrant labour system.

The basic problem was that black farmers no longer had enough land. The 'reserves'

Ai-ye! Ngana yakabona —
Ai-ye! Famine has come.
The rabbit has lost its child.
(Tonga song)[8]

The crowded reserves

which had been created in different parts of the country were too small. We have already seen that most of the land had been lost through conquest. Laws such as the Land Act of 1913 'squeezed' the black farmers even more, by preventing

them from using land outside the reserves. As a result the reserves became very crowded. There was simply not enough land to support the people living there. And there was even more pressure on the men to become wage-earners — migrant workers.

PEOPLE OF THE RESERVES

As more and more men left home to become migrant workers, life changed for those who stayed at home. Women, children, the sick and the old remained at home. They had to take over the men's jobs and look after the affairs of the family.

The land had to be cultivated.
Taxes had to be paid.
Children had to be cared for.
The sick had to be nursed.
The dead had to be buried.

The women worked the hardest. But it did not matter how hard women, old people or children worked — there was too little land. The soil got poorer and poorer.

To make things worse, as soon as the young boys were old enough to take over their fathers' work, they, too, left home to look for work in the towns.

THE CIRCLE OF POVERY

As the years passed, the reserves did not develop. Factories, big shops and cities did not grow in the reserves. Neither did rich farms. In fact, the reserves became poorer.

What happened to the reserves therefore was that:

1. Men had to get jobs as migrant workers outside the reserves, to help the families. They needed to do this because there was not enough land to feed the people.

2. The women and old people who were left could not farm as productively without the help of the strong, young and hardworking men.

3. The land they were farming was poor already because of overcrowding. The soil produced less food; thin cows produced less milk.

4. Families started to buy food, tools and clothes from the trading stores — 50 years earlier they would have produced these things themselves. Now they paid money to the storekeeper for them — and he paid the suppliers in the towns and cities. Apart

THE CIRCLE OF POVERTY IN THE RESERVES

1. The men leave home to work as migrants in the towns and mines outside the reserves.

2. Women and old people look after the land.

3. The land gets poorer.

4. Families start buying their food and clothes. Factories in the towns send manufactured goods to trading stores in the reserves.

5. The family rely more and more on money for their daily needs.

from the storekeeper's profit, money did not stay in the reserves for long.

5. So we can see why families began to rely more and more on money. When the men came back from the mines (and some did not come back at all) they did not stay for long. They had to go back to earn more money. **They were in the grip of the circle of poverty.**

30

LABOUR RESERVES

What then were the 'reserves'?

1. They were places where the children were brought up. When they were old enough, many could find jobs in the mines or the towns as migrant workers.

2. The families in the reserves looked after the people who were too sick or too old to work for wages.

3. The reserves were places where men could live with their families — when they were not working for wages.

4. They were places where women lived in separation from their husbands.

5. The reserves were places for those who had no jobs. They were places of waiting for work. They were places of labour supply for the mines and the factories.

And so, as the mines and factories got richer from the system of migrant labour, so the reserves became poorer. The reserves were no longer the farming lands which fed all the people.

The reserves became reserves of labour.

EMAKHAYA

Go, let us go my friends, go home.
Go, let us go to see our little hills.
We've long been working on the mines,
We long have left our homes for this, the place of
gold.

When we get home they will be waiting there,
Our Mothers happy when we come inside,
At Mazandekeni, home, my home.

Return my brother, from the place of gold.
Reject the town.
Cherish your mother, children and your own.
They'll clap their hands for joy
When you come home,
At home where they are waiting.
Come, come home.
(Zulu song).[7]

The two of us Mother, will pine on the mine
dumps.
But we will meet again at the Ntombela Pass.
(Zulu song).[8]

Chapter Eight
Labour Recruitment

This chapter continues the story of how the mines got their labour. We have already seen how black farmers were weakened by the loss of land, and how they had to work for wages to pay for taxes. Yet the labour shortage continued.

This chapter describes why and how the mine-owners organised a system of collecting labourers from all over southern Africa and made quite sure that these migrants reached the gold mines. This was the system of *labour recruiting*.

'At the Transvaal borders and for the succeeding hundred miles (there is) scarcity of food and shelter; from the borders to the Rand, on all the main foot paths, can be seen the evidences of this evil; skeletons of those who died are frequently seen, and at almost every store and dwelling near the road can be found those whom sickness or fatigue has compelled to give up the road and to either find a friend or perish.' (Extract from the Chamber of Mines Annual Report, 1894.)

**'The black people are crying because of taxes.
The end will be that we will just die on the road.'** (Chopi Song.)[1]

In the early years, travelling to the Witwatersrand was dangerous, especially for blacks.

The distances were great, and most blacks travelled on foot. They had to walk many miles through cold winter winds or the heavy rains of summer. Hundreds of men arrived at the Witwatersrand tired, hungry and with bleeding feet. Many men were so ill that they had to be put into hospital for a few days.

OTHER DANGERS

But natural hardships were not the only reason for the suffering of these migrant workers. Many dangers were man-made.

Along the dangerous road to the Witwatersrand mines were crooks and highway robbers, both black and white, waiting to get as much as they could from innocent black travellers.

Migrants were often arrested

Dangers on the Road

'At Viljoen's drif, trainloads of natives were given vaccinations at a fee of a shilling, passed over the river on their way to the fields and were again vaccinated on the Transvaal side at Vereeniging, this time for one shilling and sixpence (15 cents). Certificates which they had received at the drif were destroyed and new ones supplied, for a further shilling fee.'[2] In this way, officials and policemen made extra money for themselves from black migrants on their way to the mines.

In 1894 a Chamber of Mines report complained:

'It is in many places the custom of the farmers forcibly to stop any native found resting or sleeping on their farms. If these natives are coming to the (mine) fields, and have no money in their possession, they are compelled to work without payment for a few days before being allowed to proceed.'

'Natives on their way home from the East Coast to the Witwatersrand mines are being turned back by the police and sent to work on the Transvaal section of the Delagoa railway.'

'Many travel without a pass, not having the necessary shilling to buy one, and are forced to work for their greatest foes, the Boers and the railway construction contractors, who do not, we are told, scruple to use the sjambok freely, and often refuse to pay the natives even after three or four months' service.'[3]

by Free State or Transvaal police and made to pay a fine before they could continue along their way. Often, these fines went into the policemen's pockets. Other whites would pretend to be government officials on the road. They would demand money for 'taxes', or they would pretend that the migrants had done something wrong and make them pay a 'fine'.

In those days migrant workers had to pay a shilling, (ten cents) for a travel pass. Sometimes these migrants were stopped by white employers who tore up their passes and forced them to work for new passes. They also had to buy goods from these crooks.

Some crooks pretended to be policemen and demanded two pounds (about four Rand) from each traveller for passing through a 'small pox area'. Others pretended to be doctors and gave 'vaccinations' costing a shilling each.

Many blacks knew that they were being crooked and robbed. But it seems that most of them felt that they would not be able to win against these crooks. They could never be sure whether they were being robbed by real government officials and policemen or not.

Some migrants never reached the mines at all. They were kidnapped on the way by Free State and Transvaal farmers who were looking for cheap labour.

When the traveller reached the mines at last, he still had the worry of the dangerous journey back home. Miners carried their wages and presents for the family. People were robbed and even killed by gangs who lived in the veld and the koppies of the Transvaal. These robbers lived on what they could steal from passers-by.

THE TOUT SYSTEM

The Chamber of Mines was very worried about these stories of what was happening to migrant workers. They realised that people were not willing to take

---

NOTICE
To Strong Boys

I wish to make it publicly known that Sesioana of Maseru and myself have stopped flogging at Picaninny Kimberley Compound, Pretoria. Today it is your time to earn money. Wages are from 3/- to 12/- a day, according to your strength. I shall pay Hut-tax for you and shall also pay railway fares for you to Maseru to 'picanniny Kimberley'. I can also get good work at 'New Rietfontein' where you may receive wages from £3 to £6 a month. I shall also pay Hut-tax and railway fares for you from Maseru to 'New Rietfontein'. We have agreed together with the compound managers that if a person is sick he must be sent home with the Company's money and the railway fare to Maseru; they have thus bound themselves. Now my friends it is time for you to come to your friend in order to understand. The cattle have udders, come and milk them![4]

On the way to the mines.

the dangerous road to the mines, and the shortage of labour would get worse.

In 1890 an article in the Chamber of Mines Annual Report advised: 'The supply of native labour would be much improved if the difficulties met with by the kaffirs in the course of their long overland journeys, could be done away with.'

From 1889 — 1899 the mine-owners tried out a system of paying agents to bring black workers to the mines. These agents were called 'touts' But the tout system was not a success.

Touts were paid R2 or R2,50 for every worker they sent to the mines. These touts were so eager to collect their pay that they often lied to the men in the villages. They made promises to the men to get them to leave home and work for the mines. They promised them high wages and good working conditions. (We shall see in a later chapter what these working conditions were really like.) To this day, in Lesotho, touts are called *dikala-tšane*, or 'deceivers'.[5]

Many blacks complained about this trickery to the district commissioner when they got home again. For example, one district commissioner in the Cape reported:

'Native Madave along with 28 other workers at the City and Suburban mine was promised three pounds and ten shillings a month. They received only one pound and fifteen shillings.'[6] In other words, they got half of what they were promised.

The Chamber of Mines began to realise that the gold mines were getting a bad name with many blacks.

'The touts have only one object,' said one Chamber of Mines report, *'(that is) to collect "boys" in order to deliver them to companies at the highest obtainable premium. Later, the native finds he has been deceived with regard to wages, which are often far below what the tout promised, and naturally becomes discontented; but for this he blames, not the tout, but the mines; and makes the fact speedily known in the district from which he came.'*[7]
* The Chamber of Mines also realised that touts were cheating the mine-owners as well.

'A few of the powerful companies spend thousands a year in paying touts who seize upon natives actually on their road here, and get paid ten shillings or one pound per (person) for escorting them to the mine. Touts do not bring a single boy here. There is an abundance of labour in this country and it is our duty to induce that extra labour to come, and not to

fritter away thousands every year in escorting boys who were coming anyhow. '8

Mine-owners were paying the touts a lot of money to help ease the shortage of labour, yet the tout system seemed to be making things worse. The shortage of labour continued.

'SHORTAGE' OF CHEAP LABOUR

There was one main reason why the mines were always short of labour. The wages of mine labourers were lower than the wages of other labourers. The railways, the municipalities, factories and the diamond mines all paid higher wages than the gold mines. Migrants would often make their way to the mines, but find better paid jobs before they got there.

The Chamber of Mines realised this — but they insisted that they could not afford to raise the wages of unskilled workers. So the shortage of mine labour continued.

The shortage of labour brought two problems to the mine-owners.
* The first problem was that there were not enough workers to produce the gold that was in the mines as fast as the mine-owners required.
* The second problem was that unskilled workers were beginning to get higher wages. Some mines began to offer unskilled workers higher wages than other mines, to get them to come and work for them.

The tout system had failed to ease the shortage of labour on the mines. So the Chamber of Mines decided to organise its own system of collecting labour. The mine-owners realised that:

The long, and dangerous journey to Egoli. The Chamber of Mines set up their own recruiting system to make sure that workers arrived safely on the Rand and were directed to the gold mines.

* they could get more workers to the mines by making sure that they travelled safely;
* these workers would cost the mine-owners less because they would not have to pay commission to the touts;
* they would also be able to control the wages of these workers because they would all be recruited by one organisation. This would end competition amongst the mine-owners who had been forcing wages upwards.
* they would be able to direct workers to the mines where they were most needed;
* and, most important of all, the recruiting system would stop migrants from getting offers of higher pay from other employers outside the gold industry.

THE RECRUITING SYSTEM

Listen, they are off to their kraals as they are afraid they be signed on.
Chopi song about WNLA[9]

In 1901 the Chamber of Mines set up a recruiting organisation known as the Witwatersrand Native Labour Association (or WNLA). The WNLA sent agents

to villages all over Southern Africa, as far north as Zambia, Tanzania and Malawi, along the east coast of Mozambique, and also to Lesotho, Swaziland and Botswana. (In 1912, the Chamber of Mines also started the Native Recruiting Corporation. The NRC recruited blacks from within South Africa.)

Each WNLA agent would move into a little hut near the largest villages and send a 'native runner' to visit all the village men and try to get them to join the mines. Many of these runners had worked for touts before, so they were experienced in the ways of 'smooth talking'. (See the copy of a pamphlet handed out to Lesotho farmers in 1906 in the box on page 33.)

WNLA agents offered to pay the taxes of farmers to the government and also give them cash in advance. Then the farmers could work off the money they owed to WNLA by working in the mines.

WNLA also used the help of the chiefs to recruit workers. It was well known that WNLA spent some of their money on 'presents' for chiefs. The chiefs would then order the young men to join the mines. The queen of Swaziland, for example, was

---

A Dubious Doctor

A native Labour Commissioner reported this story in 1894 when he was visiting the reserves:

'The chief assured me that only a short time ago a gentleman put in an appearance styling himself "doctor", though having . . . no diploma whatever. He stated that he was authorised by the Government to vaccinate the tribe. As the bulk of the men had already been vaccinated, some (cheated) of the fee as many as three times, they declined, at the same time saying "We suppose you only want the shilling". They then proceeded to collect a number of shillings, which satisfied the visitor, and he left without vaccinating a single individual.'[10]

given thirty pounds a month as a regular 'present' for sending men to the WNLA agents.

So with the help of the government's taxes, the 'runners' and many of the chiefs, WNLA managed to set up a more efficient system of recruiting labour for the mines.

TRAVELLING TO THE MINES

When each WNLA office had collected enough men, they would all have to walk to the nearest station, which might be hundreds of miles away. WNLA officers would travel with the migrant workers, stopping at rest camps each night. Then trains would carry hundreds of workers to the WNLA centre in Germiston. The trains were often crowded and without proper toilets. Most of the journeys took a long time in those days. In 1905, for example, the train from the Mozambique border carried 2 000 men. The journey took 26 hours.

Workers from Tete, Malawi and Zambia walked to the nearest port from where they travelled by boat to Lourenco Marques (now Maputo). Others walked part of the way, passing round the borders of Zimbabwe, then travelling by train through Botswana. From Mafeking they walked to Krugersdorp, stopping at five rest camps on the way.

It was a long and tiring journey. When they reached Germiston, the mines' own doctors found that at least one out of every eight workers was in no condition to start working. But WNLA were satisfied: they had managed to get labourers to the mines. Policemen, white farmers and other employers could not stop them so easily because WNLA agents were with them.

RESULTS

The Chamber of Mines set up the recruiting system to try to stop the labour shortage on the mines and to control the wages of

The Role of the Chiefs in Recruiting

The chiefs had to play a double role in industrial times.

On the one hand, they were the traditional protector of their people. On the other hand, they were subjects of the state and could not afford to 'make trouble', otherwise they could be deposed. Many chiefs were also in the pay of WNLA as recruiting officers.

The chief's traditional influence over his people was very useful to the mines. For example, if a chief ordered a whole age group to go to the mines, it was very difficult for an individual to refuse.

On the other hand, some chiefs tried to protect the mine labourers. In 1930 one WNLA agent reported that: 'the Angoni chiefs (in Mozambique) say that they can readily send 35 000 men to work in the Transvaal only if: food is more plentifully supplied; "brothers" are not separated; they are under the supervision of someone they trust, who knows them, their language and their ways.'[11]

labourers. How far did the system succeed? The Chamber of Mines had good reason to be satisfied:

* The recruiting system did not stop the labour shortage completely, but it did manage to bring to the mines thousands of men from other countries. Recruited labour did a lot to lessen the mines' labour shortage.

* The Chamber of Mines also benefited another way from 'foreign' migrants. They came from so far away that they were prepared to stay on the mines for up to 12 months before they took the long journey back home again. This pleased the mine-owners because they saved on recruiting expenses if workers stayed on the mines for a long time.

* The recruiting system also stopped competition amongst the mines for labourers. Most of of the mining companies joined WNLA and all agreed to pay the same low wage to their labourers. So the recruiting system kept the wages down.

On the other hand there was also criticism of the system.

* Other employers pointed out that the recruiting system prevented the workers from choosing where they wanted to work. WNLA sent the workers to the mines that needed them most. Usually it was the most

unpopular mines, where the workers were badly treated, that needed workers most. Other employers resented the increasing control of the labour supply by the mine-owners.

* The wages of black South Africans were undercut by the influx of labourers from outside the country. Blacks complained that the system prevented mineworkers from bargaining for better wages. 'We say,' said a Transvaal Native Congress leader Mr S. Msimang, 'that the natives in the Union (of South Africa) are not in a position to ask for better pay, because the mines have an immense gang of cheaper labour elsewhere outside the Union.'[12]

The recruiting system, therefore, united the mine-owners and gave them more control over their workers. Black farmers were already weakened by the loss of their land and the heavy burden of taxation. The recruiting system of the Chamber of Mines made sure that many of these farmers went to the mines. They sent agents to the villages and lent farmers money to pay for their taxes and debts. Then they travelled with them all the way to the Rand to make quite sure that they would work for the mines, and not for other employers.

Chapter Nine

How the Mines got their Labour
The Contract System

Eighty years ago, all black workers in South Africa worked under a contract system. The contract system was first introduced in 1856 in the Cape as a law called the *Master and Servants Act.* Later it was copied by the Transvaal to control farm labourers and workers in the towns.

The Master and Servants Act aimed to protect both the employer and the employee in a job. It said that no worker could work without a contract. The contract had to state the following: how long the job would take; what the job would be; the worker's wage for the job.

If the worker broke his contract he could be arrested and fined or sent to jail. A worker broke his contract if he left his job or did not do his job properly, or if he was 'cheeky' or 'made a disturbance on his master's property'. If he did any of these things he was breaking his contract. He was committing a 'crime'. Employers could get into trouble too. Sometimes an employer was fined for not giving his worker his wages, or for beating him very badly. But most of the time, if there was a disagreement between an employer and his employee, it was the worker who got into trouble.

A scene at Turffontein Road Station, 1917. Workers arrive to begin their contracts on the mines.

CONTRACTS FOR THE MINES

The contract system was also used on the Kimberley diamond fields in the Cape. When the mines opened on the Witwatersrand, mine-owners again used the contract system to hire black labourers. At first the contracts lasted for about two months. Then, when deep-level mining started, the mines began to need thousands more unskilled labourers.

The mining companies tried to get longer contracts. In 1912, South African workers had to do at least 90 shifts. In 1918 the mines raised the contracts to 180 shifts (about seven months) and then in 1924 to 270 shifts (about ten months).

Mine-owners and managers wanted to keep these workers as long as possible, but many migrant workers refused to stay away from their homes for longer than half a year. They wanted to get back to their land and their families, especially during the ploughing season.

So WNLA started to find cheap labour from other countries. WNLA required all workers from outside 'British South Africa' to sign a contract of 313 shifts or more. That meant a contract of at least 12 months. WNLA claimed that they went to a lot of trouble to bring workers safely to the mines from faraway countries. The mining companies had to pay for the costs of WNLA. They had to pay for the

This poem written by Gouveia de Lemos, a Mozambiquan, describes the agony of leaving to work the long contract far away from home.

SONG OF AGONY

'Vê nerá, né 'Verá' cufä?'
I put on a clean shirt
and go to work my contract
* Which of us*
*   which of us will come back?*
Four and twenty moons
not seeing women
not seeing my ox
not seeing my land
* Which of us*
*   which of us will die?*
I put on a clean shirt
and go to work my contract
to work far away.
I go beyond the mountain
into the bush
where the road ends
and the river runs dry.
* Which of us*
*   which of us will come back?*
* which of us*
*   which of us will die?*
Put on a clean shirt
it's time to work the contract.
Get into the wagon, brother
we must travel night and day.
* Which of us*
*   which of us will come back?*
* which of us*
*   which of us will die?*
Which of us will come back
to see women
to see our lands
to see our oxen?
* Which of us will die?*
* which of us?*
* which of us?*
Which of us

The penalty for breaking the contract was prison.

WNLA offices all over southern Africa. They also had to pay the wages of the WNLA people employed to recruit labour. The mines wanted to make sure that they would get their money back by keeping these workers as long as possible. In fact, most of the men recruited by WNLA stayed on the mines for 18 months.

TWELVE-MONTH CONTRACTS

The twelve-month contract was more profitable to the mines than the six-month contract.

(1) Labourers who worked on the mines for 12 to 18 months gained more experience and learnt to work faster and better. Their work was more productive. Yet these experienced workers were paid the same as the new workers — so the mines, not the workers, profited from their experience.

(2) If a worker stayed on the mines for a long time, the mining company would not have to spend more money looking for a new worker to take his place.

(3) WNLA managed to recruit so many workers from outside

British South Africa that the shortage of labour was eased. The Chamber of Mines was able to keep wages down. As long as they could find people to work in the mines, they did not have to raise the wages.

(4) The 12 — 18 month contracts helped the mines during the ploughing season. The mines' biggest labour shortage was in the winter time, between February and May and again in December, when the workers went home again.

THE NATIVE LABOUR REGULATIONS ACT — 1911

In 1911 the South African government passed a law called the Native Regulations Act. It is interesting to study this law because it shows us what conditions must have been like for many workers. The law tried to stop some of the worst ill-treatment of black workers in the mines, on the farms and in the towns.
* The law laid down all compound managers had to be licensed. This was meant to stop some of the worst types of people being allowed to run

compounds.
* Workers had to be paid their wages in cash;
* The contract had to be written down and explained to the worker in the presence of a magistrate, so that he knew what to expect from his job.
* The law laid down the number of people allowed to sleep in any room of a certain size. This was meant to stop unhealthy overcrowding.
* The law laid down the minimum amount of food that a worker could be given at work;
* The employer had to see that a sick worker received some medical care.

But in spite of this law, conditions still remained poor. The law did not really allow the workers enough food and the compound rooms still remained cold and crowded. In any case, the government did not appoint enough inspectors to check the worst mining compounds and force them to improve conditions.

Nevertheless, some improvements were made and the law showed that the government did realise that it had a responsibility to see that black workers got at least a few basic rights.

REGULATION MEANT CONTROL

Employers continued to be happy to employ black labourers. 'The Native Regulations Act,' said economist Sheila van der Horst, 'has made the employment of Native labour more attractive.' (*Native Labour in South Africa* — 1942.) It gave employers, especially mining companies, greater control over their workers.

* Under the contract system, a worker had to stay on the mines until the manager was satisfied that he had finished his contract.

The worker had to satisfy the manager that he had done all his shifts properly before he could leave the compound. If he was ill and lost a few days' work, he had to stay on the job until his shifts were done.

* If a worker was unhappy about his working conditions he could not leave. Often, workers complained that they had not realised what the job was like before they started work. For example, many workers did not want to work underground. Yet because of the contract system they could not leave before they had worked for the period of time laid down.

* Under the contract system a black worker could not go on strike. Unlike the white worker he could not bargain for better wages and working conditions — what was a right for the white worker, was a crime for the black worker.

So, for as long as a worker's contract lasted, the employer had control over him. The worker had to continue his work without improvements in wages or conditions. He had to stay with the job until his contract was finished, or go to prison.[1]

TUBUKE KU KAYA

I want to go home,
I'm wasting my time here.
I don't want to stay,
I'd rather desert.
Please, boss,
Give me my money,
I want to go home.

(Rhodesian mine song.)[2]

CONTRACT WORKERS FROM MOZAMBIQUE

Most of the workers recruited by WNLA came from the East Coast, or Mozambique. They were popular with the mining companies because they were long-term workers. So it was not surprising that the Chamber of Mines reported that the 12-month contract 'greatly increases the value to the mining industry of the East Coast Native.' By 1910, more than half of the black mine workers on the Witwatersrand gold mines came from Mozambique. They continued to be the most important supply of labour to the mines until Mozambique became independent in 1975, when the Frelimo government stopped sending men to the South African gold mines.

Chapter Ten

How the Mines got their Labour
The Pass Laws

The pass law is perhaps the harshest single law experienced daily by thousands of Africans in today's apartheid system. Yet it goes back long before the present government came into power. What is the pass law and how did it start? This chapter traces the history of pass laws and shows how they were used by the mining industry to control labour.

The last chapter described how the contract system helped to control the supply of labour to the mines. After a worker was recruited, he would have to sign a contract, undertaking to stay on the mines until his contract expired. If he broke his contract and left his job, or if he stopped working without permission, he could be jailed.

'DESERTION'

Nevertheless, thousands of workers broke their contracts.

They left the mines because of the low pay, the bad conditions in the compounds and the dangers of working underground.

They left because under the contract system workers could not improve their working conditions or their pay. They were not allowed to bargain for improvements. They were not allowed to strike. So, many did the next best thing — they left and went to look for better jobs.

Some of the workers who left went home again. Many were caught, punished and sent back to the mines. But many were not found again. The mine-owners and the police did not always know where the workers came from or where to look for them.

When workers left their jobs, mine-owners called it *desertion*. They complained that it was no use having a contract system that

made 'desertion' a crime if the people who broke the contracts were not caught and punished. They demanded 'pass laws'.

EARLY PASS LAWS

Pass laws were not new. The first pass laws were introduced more than 200 years ago, in 1760, and applied to slaves in the Cape. Then, in 1809, the Governor of the Cape made a law which said that all 'Hottentots' had to live in one place. If they moved, they had to have a pass. By 1827, all Africans who came from outside the Cape had to have a pass.

These laws were introduced to

39

control the movement of people into the Cape Colony. This was an early form of the *influx control* that we know today.

There were also pass laws in Natal, the OFS and the Transvaal. But it was not until the discovery of diamonds in Kimberley that pass laws were fully enforced on Africans in the Transvaal.

Farm labourers began to leave the white farms to go to Kimberley. The wages on the diamond fields were higher and they were paid in cash. (On the farms, workers were paid mainly in crops.) White farmers were worried about losing their workers. They had to find ways to stop them from moving away.

TRANSVAAL PASS LAWS

In 1870, the Transvaal government made a 'one shilling' pass law. Africans who left the Transvaal had to pay a shilling to get a pass — and this was worth a lot to people who hardly ever saw money. Anyone caught leaving the Transvaal without a pass would go to jail.

Two years later, the Volksraad — the Transvaal government — passed an even stricter law to keep Africans working on the land of the Boers. Those who left the Transvaal now had to pay one pound two shillings and six pence (R2,25) for a pass.

In those days, the Transvaal was controlled by white farmers, the Boers, and the Volksraad made laws mainly for their benefit. It made these pass laws to stop people leaving their farms.

'The whole intention of the pass laws is to have a hold on the native whom we have brought to the mines, be it from the East Coast, South or from the North, at considerable outlay to ourselves.'

— Chamber of Mines.[1]

'The Pass law is nothing but slavery and forced labour. It was made to force the natives to work.'
— D.S. Letanka, Transvaal Native Congress.[2]

PASSES ON THE MINES

After gold was discovered in the Transvaal, the government made much money by taxing the mines. The Volksraad was still controlled by Boers, but they realised the value of the mines. They were ready to help the mine-owners to get the cheap labour that they wanted.

Deep-level mining needed far more cheap labour. In 1896, the year deep-level mining began, the Volksraad passed two laws to help the mine-owners control the supply and movement of black miners.
* The first law was a stricter pass law. It said: 'All Natives on the Rand must be in the employ of a master and wear a metal plate or badge on the arm in token of such employ.' If an African man did not have a badge, it meant that he was not employed, so he should not be on the Witwatersrand. He could be arrested and imprisoned, or forced to work.
* The second law divided the gold mining areas into *labour*

districts. When an African entered a labour district he had to get a *district pass*. This district pass allowed him to stay for three days to look for work. If he had not accepted a job within three days, he had to leave that labour district and look for work in another district where labour was short.

With these additions to the pass laws, the mine-owners hoped to control the thousands of unskilled workers on the mines. They hoped that the pass system would stop desertions and channel workers to the mines that were short of labour.

The new laws restricted the freedom of black workers to choose jobs — they could be forced to work in areas that were inconvenient and on mines where working conditions were known to be particularly harsh.

STRICTER PASS LAWS: LOWER WAGES

In 1897, a year after the stricter pass laws were introduced, the Chamber of Mines decided to cut the wages of black miners. All the gold mines agreed to pay unskilled workers a fixed, low wage. No mine would pay more than 12 cents a shift for surface work. The most any unskilled underground worker could ever get was 25 cents a shift.

The Chamber of Mines expected trouble after they had forced wages down. They asked the government to send extra police to guard the mines and the compounds.

Johannesburg Pass Office, 1903.

PASS OFFICE

Take off your hat.
What is your name?
Who is your father?
Who is your chief?
Where do you pay your tax?
What river do you drink?

We mourn for our country.

(Zulu song.)[3]

Serial No.   Form 1 L.

NATIVES LABOUR IDENTIFICATION PASSPORT.   IN CASE OF RENEWAL OR EXCHANGE OF EMPLOYER.

REGISTERED

Nº · 23303   A. District JOHANNESBURG.

1 Name (Native) *Charlie Mfelasi*
2 Name known by *Charlie*
3 Father's Native Name *Ngwanki*
4 Tribe or Nationality *Baca Makowla*
5 Place of Residence *Mzimklanga.*
    Mc Alibb J.C.
6 Travelling to
7 In charge of

Pass Officer JOHANNESBURG
9. 2. 03.

The Pass

The pass was a document of labour control. Any white or policeman could stop an African and ask to see his pass. When he looked at the pass he would find:
* the name and address of the bearer, as well as his father's name and his chiefdom, so that the bearer could easily be traced if he ran away or commited a 'crime';
* the name of the district where the pass owner was allowed to look for work;
* the date on which the pass was issued — the pass bearer had only six days to find a job, otherwise he had to try for another district. This method made sure that labour was directed to the areas where it was most needed;

* the names and addresses of all the employers of the pass bearer, past and present; how long he had worked for each of them; what kind of work he had done and what the employer thought of him (in the character reference, at the back of the document). In addition, the pass bearer's wages for each job were recorded. The job seeker was therefore at the mercy of all his employers. What they said about him decided whether he would get a job in the future. The wage he had been paid in the past decided the wage that he would be paid in the future.

All the information on the pass was also registered in the files at the Pass Office, making it easier to keep track of all workers. Notice that desertion had to be reported to the Pass Office, so that the deserter could be caught and punished for breaking his contract.

Black miners responded in the only way they could: as wages fell, desertion rose.

In the mines of the Robinson Company, for example, after the wages dropped 1 600 workers deserted in less than a year. Not one was caught and brought back to work on the mines.

Again, in 1897, figures showed that 14 000 Africans deserted from 33 mines — and again, not one was brought back.

The mine-owners blamed the government for not employing enough policemen to check passes and arrest deserters. One mine-owner, S. Jennings, complained to a government commission in 1897 that it was possible to keep down the wages of unskilled workers only if the government helped to control the workers. He said:

'We have a most excellent law, namely the pass law, which should enable us to obtain complete control over the kafirs. (But) the Pass Law gives us no such protection . . . As the matter now stands, we import kafirs who sign a contract to serve us for 12 months; many leave after a couple of weeks and

it is impossible to recover them.'[4]

Another mine-owner, Sir Percy Fitzpatrick, said, *'We cannot maintain the new rate unless the government helps us in carrying out the Pass Law.'[5]*

Soon afterwards, in 1899, Britain went to war against the Boer republics of the Transvaal and the Orange Free State. What became known as the Anglo-Boer War lasted nearly four years. (Chapter 12 deals more fully with this subject.) Most of the mine-owners supported the war and were very happy when the British won it.

TWO VIEWS OF THE PASS SYSTEM

'The pass system protects them (black workers) against unscrupulous employers and when a dispute over length and conditions of service arises. Also in the event of accident or death it makes it possible to inform relatives and remit money.'
Government official, 1919.

'A passport is supposed to be a protection to natives and re-garded as an agreement made at the Pass Office between the employer and the employee. Questions: (1) If so, why should I be compelled to carry this agreement or document with me? (2) Why should police run after me day and night asking me to produce this document and cause me to be absolutely restless? (3) Why can't I place it in my box for safety?'
— Member of the Transvaal Native Congress,1919.[6]

After the war, the new British governor tightened up the laws to help the mine-owners to get more workers for the mines, and to control them. He also 'modernised' the pass system. Instead of the old metal badge, the pass became a signed document, giving full details of the worker's history. The worker had to carry his pass at all times if he was not either at work or at home. This made it easier to keep track of every African worker. At the same time, the governor enlarged the police force to make sure that the pass system was effective, and that 'offenders' were caught and punished.

THE FUNCTION OF THE PASS

A pass was many things: it was special permission to look for work in a certain district; the monthly pass was a record of a man's background and history; it showed if he was employed, where and for what wage; it showed whether he had ever been convicted of a crime, however small; it indicated that he had paid his taxes (otherwise he would not have been given a pass at all); and it also gave a character reference by his previous employers.

The photograph on page 41 shows the monthly pass.

There were other passes too.

1. **The Six-day pass** gave a work-seeker permission to look for work in a particular district for six days only. This period included weekends and public holidays. After six days, if he had not found employment, the work-seeker had to leave the district, or break the law.

2. **A travelling pass** was also required if a man wanted to leave his home and travel to another district to find a job. He had to pay a shilling fee for this pass.

3. **Night passes** had to be carried by any black person who was out in a municipal area after 9.00 p.m. These were signed by the employer.

4. **A 'special' pass** had to be carried when a worker left his employer's premises, even for a few hours. The 'special' was directed at black mine-workers who left the compounds.

Any white man or policeman could stop an African and ask to see his pass. If the pass was not in order, the 'wrong-doer' could be arrested. Any desertions had to be reported to the Pass Office, so that the deserter's records could be traced, making it easier for him to be caught.

'PASSES PREVENT MONEY'

'At our meeting at Vrededorp on 30 March 1919, we came to the conclusion that passes prevent money.'
— Transvaal Native Congress pamphlet, 1919.[7]

In 1899, the Chamber of Mines had demanded 'a complete system of control over the natives at the mines, so that they could be traced from place to place from the date of their arrival on the fields to that of their departure.'[1]

The British governor's new pass system after the war gave the mine-owners good reason to be satisfied.

'We are now able to deal with our mines and other enterprises in this country as one would naturally deal with these undertakings,' said mine-owner Sir Percy Fitzpatrick in a speech to the shareholders of Rand Mines in 1903.[8]

And because the pass system increased employers' control over their workers in a number of ways, it served to maintain an obedient work force — the character reference could prevent a man from being employed again, as could the 'criminal' stamp if he broke his contract. 'Troublemakers' could be endorsed out and lose their jobs and passes for ever. In addition, the six-day pass deprived a man of the time he needed to find the highest pay or the best job — he had to take what he could get (usually on the mines). Passes restricted workers to certain labour districts, so that they were not free to move to where the best jobs were.

In short, the pass system:
* restricted freedom of movement by directing workers where employers needed cheap labour;
* enforced the contract system by making sure that they stayed there as long as they were wanted;
* policed the workers and 'weeded out' the unemployed;
* further weakened the position of the black labour force;
* and in so doing, helped to maintain a cheap labour system.

The control of labour through the system of pass laws continues in South Africa to this day.

42

Chapter Eleven
The Compound System

At the end of the long road to the mines the strange and harsh life of the compound-dweller awaited the black worker.

Dispossessed of his land, needing money to pay taxes, brought to the mines by WNLA and made to stay there by the pass and the contract, the worker found himself a virtual prisoner in the compound; for the compound system imposed almost total control on him while he was at the mine.

In this chapter we try to give an idea of what life in the compounds must have been like. Then we analyse the system itself.

THE FIRST COMPOUNDS

Compounds were not new to South Africa. Mine-owners had developed the compound system in the diamond mines of Kimberley. There, all the workers were housed in large buildings next to the mines, where workers ate and slept together. They were carefully watched and controlled to prevent diamond stealing.

Mine-owners on the Rand were quick to realise the benefits to the employers of compounds. We shall discuss these benefits later in the chapter.

The early compounds on the Rand were usually wood and iron shacks — 'nothing more than camps', a Native Commissioner reported in 1903.

Living conditions were mostly overcrowded, dirty and unhealthy, although some mines provided better housing than others.

Inspectors reported that the compound huts contained 20 to 50 workers, who slept on concrete bunks built one above the other like shelves. Many of the huts had earth floors which turned muddy in wet weather. When the huts were crowded, workers had to sleep on these damp floors.

In the earlier years, many compounds did not provide washing facilities, but by 1903 most compounds had concrete baths in the centre of the compound in which workers could wash themselves and their clothes.

The compounds were badly built, often with no windows or lights. Cracks in the walls were stuffed with rags to keep out the wind and the cold. The only heating came from an 'imbandla', a big tin of hot coal giving off highly dangerous smoke fumes.

There was no place for workers' possessions. Clothes, bicycles other belongings hung from the ceiling and people could only hope that these would not get stolen.

The appalling conditions in the compounds were described in dozens of reports. Here are typical comments from inspectors.

'...20 huts in the compound, being about 14 years old and practically worn out, as the smoke of the years has corroded the iron of which they are built. There are no floors to the huts, no bedsteads, no stoves, no proper ventilation and no light at night.'

— The Stubbs Gold Mine.[1]

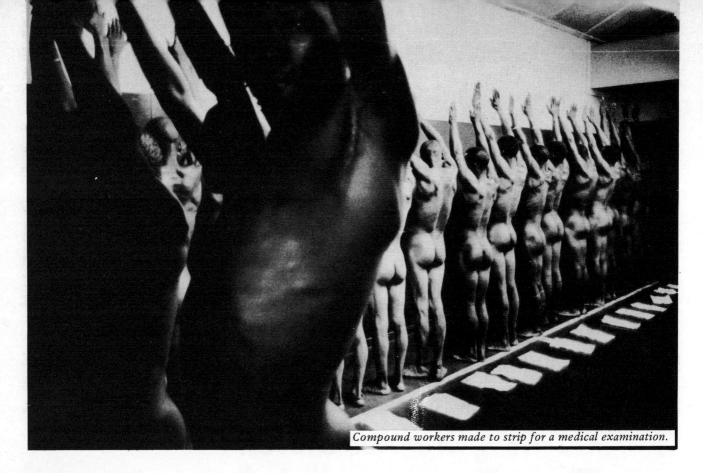

Compound workers made to strip for a medical examination.

'...Of the 50 rooms, 49 floors which are either defective or absolutely rotten...many of the labourers are obliged to sleep on the rotten uneven floors which it is not possible to clean. The boys complain of being unable to sleep owing to the unevenness of the floors and the insects.'[2]

— New Randfontein Gold Mines.

Compound conditions were generally so bad that in 1903, when Chinese workers were brought in (see Chapter 14), the British government insisted that the mines build new or improved compounds for them. After the Chinese left, nearly all black workers were housed in compounds.

Eventually, some of the richer mines 'modernised' their compounds. They built new compounds with bathing facilities, electric lights in the rooms and higher ceilings for better ventilation. Compounds were built according to a plan like the one shown below in the photograph on this page.

LIFE IN THE COMPOUNDS

Life in the compounds was very different from village life at home. In the compound, men slept on cement beds in rows, in huge crowded rooms — terribly different to the small, comfortable private huts at home!

There was no privacy anywhere in the compound. The toilets were nothing but a long bench with holes where 20 men could relieve themselves at the same time. Washing was also a public business and in the rooms, the men dressed and undressed in full view of others. The lights were left on all night.

'In the hostel there is no privacy in the rooms nor in the open lavatories nor in the shower rooms. It is against the tradition that a son sees his father naked or on the toilet. But hostel life has forcefully changed that.'

— from *Another Blanket*

FOOD

The compound was supposed to provide most of the food the workers needed to stay alive. The Chamber of Mines made an agreement with the mining companies that the rations should be the same in all the compounds — not more than 5 lbs of mealie-meal plus 2 lbs of meat a week, to save costs.

This was not enough food for doing hard manual labour for ten

A 'modern' compound. According to the Deputy Commissioner of Police in 1913, an efficient compound 'should be surrounded by a high iron fence' and have 'barbed wire on the top which prevents anybody getting in or out'. It should 'contain' the workers, have a reliable guard and a sufficient supply of arms in the manager's office.[3]

hours or more every shift. To keep up their strength, they had to buy their own food out of their low wages. A report in 1909 showed that many of the workers spent half their wages on food.

Often, compound food was not fit to eat. In 1903, a government report found rotten food served in a number of compounds. For example:

'Coarsely ground meal. Many of the particles of flour were black and purple. Slightly mouldy and musty smell. Not fit for human consumption.'
    — of a sample of mealie-meal from the Treasury Gold Mining Co.

'Small mealies, most discoloured, purple and brown in parts. The majority of the corns contained weevils. Very disagreeable and musty smell. Not fit for human consumption.'
    — of a sample of mealies from the Glencairn Gold Mining Co.[4]

Food was also used as a means of controlling labour. Only men who could show their stamped ticket were given meat and bread. A stamped ticket was supposed to show that the worker had done his assigned load of work.

SPARE TIME

In those early mining years, compound workers had very little spare time. Often, they were so tired after a shift underground that they spent their spare time sleeping. According to one compound manager, workers should either be 'working, resting or in hospital.'

The managers were chiefly concerned with one thing: to run the compound without trouble. They tended to treat the workers not as men, but as numbers. Workers were identified by the numbered bracelets they wore on their arms.

In later years, managers began to organise the spare time of the

Compound workers pose with the manager for a visiting photographer in 1899. Meals in the compound were usually inadequate, and the workers had to buy their own food to supplement their rations.

Youngsters cutting hair (above) and making ornaments (below) in their spare time. Removed from normal society, close friendships were very important. Often, a chief would send an entire 'age regiment' off to the mines, so that at least they could be together in the hostile world of the compound.

45

compound workers — 'to keep them out of trouble.' Tribal dances and competitions were arranged, one group against the other. The dancing gave many workers great pleasure and a chance to express themselves, but it also kept alive the tribal divisions in the compounds.

Compound workers were migrant workers, their families far away. In the compound, they saw only other workers. They lived in a world of men.

The compound was a place where people had little money, and pleasures were hard to find. Many workers spent their money on heavy drink or *dagga*, to forget where they were.

'If one is not drunk one is homesick.'

— A compound worker.[5]

Compound workers in a dance contest. The teams were divided along ethnic lines.

If they got a pass to leave the compound, they would spend more of their money on women.

It was hard to save money in these conditions, and hard to remember the needs of the family in the harsh world of the compound.

Liquor as a Form of Control

The supply of liquor to black workers has an interesting history.

When the gold mines first started, liquor was given to recruits to tempt them to work in the mines. Mine-owners began to invest in the liquor industry, and in the early years, many mine managers had a policy of rewarding hard workers with a 'tot' at the end of a shift. One newspaper commented that 'better work is got out of (the worker) when he sees the prospect of a cheering glass at the end of a day's labour.'[6]

The Boers also benefited from this practice, as alcohol was distilled from the crops that they sold.

The situation began to change, however, when many workers drank so much that they could not work productively. By the time managers stopped supplying liquor, workers were buying their own liquor, getting drunk at their own expense.

Mine-owners suddenly became concerned with the morals, health and safety of their workers. They began to support the campaign for the banning of liquor to black workers. But the Transvaal government resisted, because of the farmers' interests in the industry.

It was only after the Boers were defeated in the Anglo-Boer War that 'European-style' alcohol became illegal for black workers.

Policemen supervise the disposal of liquor confiscated from compounds and shebeens.

People of the Compounds

The compounds represented a carefully worked out system of control. There were people in charge at every level to watch over the workers and to make sure that the system worked smoothly.

The compound manager was in charge of the compound as well as the underground section. He was usually chosen because he could 'understand the native' — in other words, he could 'control the workers'. The compound manager wielded great power over the men, meting out punishment.

His job was so important to the mine-owners that he was put in a class above the ordinary white worker and paid much higher wages.

The induna was appointed by the compound manager. He was usually a 'boss boy' who had satisfied the manager with his good work. The induna lived in his own rooms. He received higher wages than the other black workers, and extra beer and meat. The job of the induna was to keep order amongst the workers and settle their quarrels. Some indunas saw themselves as chiefs, but often workers did not accept the induna because he was chosen by the manager. 'We don't elect him,' said one worker, 'he is appointed in the night.' 'He does not care about worker problems,' said another. 'He sides with management.' *From Another Blanket*

However, this was not always the case. Indunas sometimes acted for the workers. Early reports show many cases of indunas writing to chiefs and magistrates in their home districts to complain of bad treatment in the mine. The induna had privileges and owed his job to the compound manager but at the same time he was still a worker. His job was a difficult one, because he had to play a double game.

Compound policemen were also appointed by the compound manager. They were allowed to carry knobkerries or sticks and they guarded the compound gate and controlled the queues to the kitchen and the washing rooms. They had to wake the workers in time for the next shift.

They helped the Induna to settle quarrels, acting as his advisers or councillors. They were given the power to search rooms for stolen goods, alcohol, dagga or dangerous weapons. In many compounds they also had the power to detain workers.

Compound policemen were paid extra money for their jobs, but lived with the workers.

The Sibonda — In each room a sibonda was chosen by his room mates to keep order in the room. He would give tasks to each person in the room so that it was kept clean and tidy. The Sibonda would settle small quarrels in the room.

The sibonda was responsible to his room mates and did not get the higher wages or other privileges for his job. He spoke for his room mates if there was any complaint.

Nevertheless, the compound manager found the sibonda system useful because he could find out what was happening in the rooms if he needed to.

The workers — There were about 3 000 men in each compound. The workers were divided into three main language groups — Sotho, Xhosa and Shangaan. Workers of one language group had very little to do with other workers in the compound. They ate and slept separately.

'In many respects the compound resembles the barracks, and it becomes a simple impossibility to maintain order and discipline unless the compound manager is recognised as having considerable power.' — Editor of 'SA Mining Journal', 1894.

THE MINE POLICEMEN

An early photo of compound policemen.

Both the indunas and the policemen had some power because they were the manager's men. They had to satisfy the manager rather than the workers.

But they would sometimes play a double role — they would promise to help a worker in trouble by speaking to the manager. Usually, the worker would have to pay for this service.

It was a common practice to appoint Zulu policemen. The compound workers were divided into different language groups, but nearly all the men hated the compound police. This hatred of Zulus (and suspicion of other groups) served the managers very well. As one government official said: 'The inter-tribal jealousies have always rendered it possible, in the last resort, to protect Europeans by utilising one tribe against another.'[7]

VIOLENCE

Every compound had its detention room where workers could be handcuffed and locked up. In 1903, a government official agreed with managers that the compound jail was *an absolute essential as being the only means of controlling riotous and quarrelsome natives ... as it not infrequently happens that a native "runs amok" it is necessary that he should be promptly dealt with in order to prevent further developments.*[8]

In the mines, workers were often punished to get them to work harder. Although it was against the law, supervisors would often hit, and kick their workers. Threatening and shouting were part of the day's work. The 1913 Native Grievances Inquiry described conditions in their report:

'Natives are frequently assaulted by Europeans, generally underground. A certain number of such cases seems inevitable when the conditions of work are considered.

'The mines consist of an enormous mileage of tunnels, in which a number of Europeans, many of them of no high standard of education or ethics are in practically unchecked control of several members of a subservient race. As a rule, neither the master nor the servant understands the other's language, yet the master has to give directions and the servant to obey them.

'Both parties are working under unhealthy and unnatural conditions. In these circumstances the temptation and the opportunity for assaults on the servant by the master are constantly present; and these circumstances may perhaps be modified, but cannot be altogether removed.'[9]

Everyday violence was also used on workers by the compound policemen. They carried sjamboks in the compound. They were not supposed to use them, but they did. Underground 'boss boys' also carried them.

Great anger and bitterness built up in the unnatural crowded conditions of the compounds. Where workers were divided into ethnic groups and there was a shortage of food, liquor, women and money, people were suspicious of others. Sometimes, a small quarrel would build up and spread like wild fire through the whole compound. One group would turn against another, and there would be open battles, leaving people seriously wounded or even dead.

Working in constant danger also led to tensions underground. These tensions sometimes led to unplanned violence.

'An older man accidentally loosened a rock with his spade. It fell on the foot of a young worker below him. In great terror, the young man sprang up and struck him with the spade. The older man was taken to hospital in a serious condition.'
— From *Another Blanket*.

TWO VIEWS OF THE COMPOUND

'To the old hands this is like a club. They get away from the squabbles of the women and the domestic worries and then, just as sailors do, they go home and are received as heroes. They love it.'
— Compound Manager[10]

'Surely the miners are ill-treated all through. Not only by whites but more especially by their fellow men. That is why they have to be rough because they live in a rough situation. Any kind of soft person can hardly survive here.'
— Compound worker[11]

Ulelezindundumeni —
Lying in the graves,
Lying on the mine dumps,
The lover of my child.
(Zulu song.)[12]

The harsh life in the compounds, poor food and medical care and the dangerous work underground caused the deaths of many miners every year. Reports on the compounds show just how bad conditions were for the health of the workers.

'Crowding increases the spread of any infectious disease. This applies particularly to pneumonia, tuberculosis and cerebrospinal meningitis.'
—Medical officer to Chamber of Mines, 1914.[13]

'We were not well treated, we even had to work on Sundays, we had to load the ore trucks. We got coarse food to eat. After about two months we began to get ill. We had stomach-ache first then our feet got swollen and we could not walk. The doctor used to see us and gave medicine. Some died . . . '
— Worker on Jubilee Mine 1902.

'I found natives who should have been carefully covered up lying on the ground out of doors and the majority of them with only a very scanty covering. In the afternoon the floors were being washed and it was not reasonable to expect them to be dry before evening . . . not many of the serious cases will have a chance of recovery.'
— Dr Sansom, District Health Officer, Report on Langlaagte Compound Hospital, 1903.

'A case has come to my notice where a native was injured by a fall of rock about 9 a.m., his leg being badly broken and great loss of blood occurring. He reached the mine hospital about 11 a.m. No attempt was made to get a doctor until 1.45 p.m., after the hospital superintendent had dressed the injury. A note was then sent to the mine medical

We do not like our men to go to Johannesburg because they go there to die. (Sotho Chief)

A compound hospital. Thousands of mineworkers died each year from disease, malnutrition and accidents underground.

officer to which he replied that he could not come until 5 p.m. as he could not get an anaesthetist. The patient died, of shock and haemorrhage, at 4.50 p.m., no doctor having seen him.'
— Director of Native Labour, 1913.

In 1903, 5 022 black workers died on the mines. The causes of their deaths were:
- Pneumonia and meningitis, from crowded, damp conditions, sudden changes in temperature, and general weakness — more than half (59%);
- Intestinal infections, from bad food — 11.86%;
- Scurvy, from lack of vegetables — 5.8%;
- Accidents — 4.08%;
- Bacillosis — 5.39%;
- Tuberculosis, from sudden changes in temperature and damp conditions — 5.39%.[14]

'At the mines he must work hard, about ten hours every day, mostly underground and gets very inefficient food; as a matter of fact he has to live on mealie-meal porridge, although he is supplied with one pound of meat

twice a week and recently some mines have commenced supplying them occasionally with fresh vegetables. This does not help much. As a consequence of this bad feeding, the natives are generally weak and unhealthy, and sickness, and especially scurvy is of frequent occurrence.'
— State Mining Engineer's report, 1901.[15]

Pneumonia took the lives of many workers from hot countries like Zambia, the Congo and Tanzania. In 1911, for example, more than 67 out of every 1 000 mine-workers died of pneumonia. These figures were so shocking that in 1913 the government stopped workers from these countries being recruited to the mines. They were not used to the cold Transvaal nights. When they came up from the hot underground tunnels after a long shift, the change of air was too great for them.

'If the mines continued to employ these people it would be little less than murder.' — Minister of Native Affairs, 1913.[16]

Why Compounds?

Why were compounds set up in the gold mines? In Kimberley the compound system prevented stealing. But gold could not be stolen out of the rock in the same way as diamonds. The Rand mine-owners therefore did not need compounds to prevent stealing. Nevertheless, the compound system had so many other advantages for the diamond mine-owners that the gold mine-owners decided to use the system as well. Why was this?

CHEAP LABOUR

To understand why the compound system was used on the gold mines one must remember the aims of the mine-owners. Their aims were very different from those of the workers.

* Most workers went to the mines to earn money to support themselves and their families on the land. They needed their wages to survive.

* The mine-owners, on the other hand, wanted the mines to produce as much gold as possible — they wanted to make big profits. But gold mining in the Witwatersrand was expensive and the price of gold was fixed. To make big profits, mine-owners had to cut down on their costs — to save money somewhere.

How did they save money? The only way mine-owners could save money on their costs was to use cheap labour — and they got cheap labour by employing migrant workers.

CHEAPER LABOUR

Mine-owners paid compound workers lower wages. They were able to pay such low wages because they could argue that they housed and fed the workers in large numbers. The workers did not actually pay for living in the compounds — they received lower wages instead. So the compound system saved the mine-owners a lot of money.

It was quite cheap for the mines to provide space for large numbers of workers to sleep in. It was cheap to give them a diet of *pap* and sometimes meat (usually offal). It would cost a worker more to rent a room for himself, buy his own food and pay for transport as well.

Life in the compounds was hard. Nevertheless, the system claimed to save the workers money. It saved the mine-owners a lot more money.

MORE PRODUCTION

There was another reason why mine-owners liked the compound system. The men in compounds worked more regularly because they could be watched more carefully.

Before the compound system, more than a quarter of the workers would stay away from work on any one day but the compound system resulted in over 90 percent of the workers going to work every day.

In the compounds, fewer workers ran away. They were not allowed to leave until they had finished their contracts — contracts on the mines were usually for six to 12 months. The compounds were carefully guarded. Workers who stayed and worked for the mines for six to 12 months also became more experienced. They learnt to work more quickly — and more gold was produced.

50

CONTROL OF WORKERS

For the mine-owners, the most useful thing about the compound system was that it kept tight control of workers. If workers 'gave trouble' or tried to resist their low wages or conditions of work, it was easy for the army and the police to surround the compounds and imprison the workers with their guns.

As a government commission of enquiry advised in 1913:

'. . . steps ought certainly to be taken to render the compounds more easily convertible into places of detention. Where the compound has strong, steel-cased gates which can be locked from the outside, only one entrance, and high walls with no outer windows, a comparatively few armed men can prevent exit from it and thus isolate a disturbance which might otherwise spread with alarming conse-*quences.*'[17]

The government itself, therefore, recommended that the compounds be used as places of control and punishment, like prisons.

The compound system prevented resistance from workers in a number of ways:
* It was easier to find out who the organisers were in a compound.
* It was easier to stop workers in all the compounds from knowing that there was trouble outside the compounds.

In short, compounds:
- **separated the mineworkers from other workers;**
- **controlled the workers; and**
- **turned workers into labour machines.**
Compounds, therefore, made workers more profitable to the mine-owners.

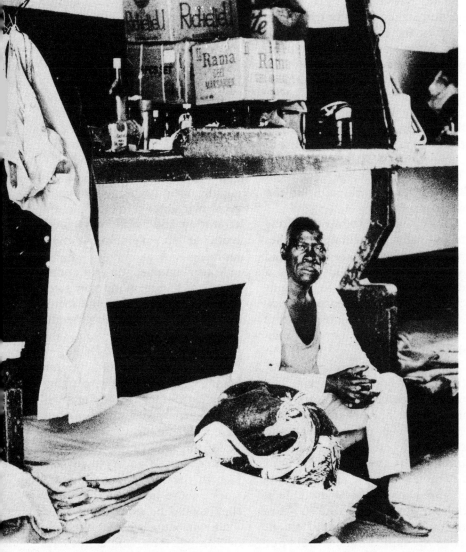

FAMILY PLANNING

Row upon row
Like winter-shaken stalks of maize,
The barracks stretch from one
Miserable end to the other.

Within the enfenced hostel
No gay children bounce and romp about,
No busy housewives colour
The washing line once a week.
Here there is no homely smell of food
That wanders in the air during the day.

Sunset gathers the half-castrated inmates
Like stale crumbs from the city.
They plod through the large gates
Weary, bent: and shut
Their fatigued minds, eyes and ears.
For them the day is over.
They are banished to a twilight life.

The silence that they left behind
At the breaking of the dawn is
Rippled as if it was a calm lake
By laughter as they buzz about
Like newly-wedded women.

They strip off to their vests
Embalmed in a day's sweat.
Yesterday's tripe and porridge are
Hastily warmed up for supper again.

One by one, they enjoy their naked
                                    showers
Splashing their rigid bodies in the water,
And return to their stuffy rooms.

An inmate belches like a sea-rover.
It echoes in the far-flung room.
He raps his full stomach
That is large as a mole-hill:
'Exchoose me you bastards!' he thunders.

They slip into their stony beds,
Clasp their baggy and sweat-reeking
Pillows as if they were their
Beloved ones left in the homelands.

They look at their shirts,
Overalls, trousers, jackets — all ragged,
Hanging aslant on the damp walls
Like faded, dusty family portraits.

Portable radios are switched off,
Candle flames flicker and die,
Darkness and silence covers
Them all like a large blanket.
Alone,
They quietly succumb to sleep.

In the night,
An inmate's untroubled sleep is
                                    interrupted.
He sits on the edge of his bed
Half dozing,
Gazing from darkness to darkness,
And then he spills the seeds of nature
All over his slovenly sheet with
                                    half-satisfaction:
'Family planning,' he whispers to himself.
Then the musical snores
Of the sleep-drowned inmates
Slowly lull him back to sleep.

James Twala[18]

Working in the Mines

INGOLOVANE

There are trucks in the mine!
They are everywhere.
They are in Kimberley and Vereeniging,
Yet their real home is in Johannesburg.

They are pushed in the mines by the strong men of
Africa.

There are trucks.
We did not sleep last night, we were working.
There are trucks,
There are trucks.

(Xhosa song)[19]

(For the mine worker the line of trucks is endless, carrying the refuse of the mills high onto the vast dumps.)

For migrant workers, life in the compounds and mines came as a great shock. Most of the migrant workers were subsistence farmers who had worked all their lives on the land, out in the open. Many had never been to a large town before.

Most workers had never seen machines before they went to the mines. They had never worked underground, in the dark, in the dust, in the terrible heat. The new workers had to learn new ways of working.

Work lost its old meaning. They were no longer working only for themselves and their families.
As migrant workers they worked for others — they worked for a wage.

In the mines, they could not work only at times when they saw work was needed, as they had done on the land. The mine owners wanted the mines to produce as much gold as possible. So the workers had to work in shifts. They worked day and night, nine, ten or more hours at a time.

A WORKING DAY UNDER-GROUND

Working conditions were not exactly the same at every mine — some were much better than others. But the working day at every mine followed more or less the same pattern:

The 'native day shift' would go down the mine any time from four to six o'clock in the morning. Some were given hot coffee, others got no food at all.

When the workers reached the level where they had to work, they were supposed to wait for the white miners to come. But the white supervisors did not come until 6.30 a.m., so the 'boss boy' would get the workers to start work without the white miner.

They would start by getting tools ready and filling up holes where yesterday's dynamite had not exploded. (This was a dangerous thing to do without checking — unexploded dynamite could explode later or cause fires, leading to terrible accidents.)

When the white miner arrived, the day's work would begin. The workers spent a few hours lashing — shovelling broken rock into trucks to be taken up to the surface. When the lashing was finished, it was time to drill new holes.

The workers hammered deep holes into the rock so that the dynamite fuse could fit in. Then the skilled miner would put in the dynamite. By this time it would be about 3 o'clock in the afternoon.

The skilled miners and the lashers, trammers and hammer men would leave. The workers who helped with the blasting of the holes would stay until they finished their work. This could take until 7 o'clock at night.

During this long working day of nine to 15 hours, labourers were not given any food. If they wanted to eat underground they had to bring their own food.

The night shift worked for equally long hours. They would go down at two o'clock in the afternoon and usually only finish work at six o'clock the next morning.

White miners, on the other hand, did not work for more than ten hours a day and in the middle of the shift they would go up to the surface for a two-hour food break. Often, a 'learner blaster' would be left behind to supervise the blasting, despite the fact that he was still learning to blast and did not yet have a certificate.

At the end of the shift, the workers would go up to the surface in the lift. After their hard work in the hot, airless tunnels, they would be sweating heavily. Even when the weather was cold or raining, they would still have

'If I go to the mines, where shall I find the courage to get into the cage?'
(From a Chopi song).[20]

Mine Boy
An Excerpt
from the Novel
by Peter Abrahams

Peter Abrahams

'For Xuma the day was strange. Stranger than any day he had ever known. There was the rumbling noise and the shouting and the explosions and the tremblings of the earth. And always the shouting indunas driving the men on to work. And over all those, the bitter eyes and hardness of the white man who had told him to push the truck when he did not know how.

It was the strangeness of it all that terrified him. And the look in the eyes of the other men who worked with him. He had seen that look before when he was at home on the farms . . . The eyes of these men were like the eyes of the sheep that did not know where to run when the dog barked. It was this that frightened him.

And when a lorry came the men jumped out of the road and ran like the sheep. Over all this the induna was like a shepherd with a spear. And the white man sat with folded arms.

With another he had pushed the loaded truck up the incline. The path was narrow on which they had to walk and it was difficult to balance well. And the white man had shouted. 'Hurry up!' And the induna had taken up the shout. And one little truck after another, loaded with fine wet white sand, was pushed up the incline to where a new mine-dump was being built.

But as fast as they moved the sand so fast did the pile grow. A truck load would go and another would come from the bowels of the earth. And another would go and another would come. So it went on all day long. On and on and on and on.

But the sand remained the same. A truck would come from the heart of the earth. A truck would go up to build the mine-dump. Another would come. Another would go . . . All day long . . .

And for all their sweating and hard breathing and for the redness of their eyes and the emptiness of their stare there would be nothing to show. In the morning the pile had been so big. Now it was the same. And the mine-dump did not seem to grow either.

It was this that frightened Xuma. This seeing of nothing for a man's work.'

Acknowledgement: Heinemann African Writers Series.

---

to wait in queues to collect their tickets, to show that they had finished another shift.

Only when they had their tickets could they at last get their food. If they had bought some food of their own to add to the small supply, they first had to cook it.

After eating, the workers would talk a little. As there was very little lighting in their rooms, there was not much else they could do. There was no chance of washing their clothes — these might get stolen during the night when they were hanging up to dry.

Usually, the tired worker would go to sleep soon after his meal, before another long, hard shift underground the next day.

ACCIDENTS

Working underground was not only hard and uncomfortable. It was also dangerous. Rock bursts and rock falls killed people regularly. In those early mining years there were even more deaths in the gold mines than there are today. In July 1903, for example, the death rate was 112 for every thousand mine-workers — some died from accidents, some from disease and others from general weakness.

Workers did not have proper working clothes and protective helmets. Danger was always with them underground.

'Working in the mines is an agonising and painful experience. Your work is in an extremely dangerous place. Whenever you go down into the shaft, you are not sure that you will come out alive. You don't want to think about it. But it keeps coming. Whenever an accident occurs and someone is either killed or badly injured, you think of yourself in that position, you think of your family and you become very unstable and lonely. You feel you want to see them for the last time . . . Death is so real you keep on praying and thanking God each time you come out alive.'
— from *Another Blanket.*

M'GODINI

I went to the country of Joana.
I find men working underground.
Working with tools in their hands
The hammer and drills of the bones
To break the rocks that are so hard
Working by candlelight.

Fire! zzi; fire, zzi!
Bad luck! The holes are blasted
It kills men underground.

(Shangaan song.)[21]

Chapter Twelve

The Wage Colour Bar—
A System of Forced Labour

As capitalists, and with the fixed price of gold, mine-owners were concerned to keep their expenses low and production high. This chapter shows how the mine-owners used their power to keep black workers' wages low while extracting as much work out of them as possible.

MORE WORK FOR LOWER WAGES

The mine-owners made their profits by establishing the system of the wage colour bar. But there was another way that mine-owners could increase their profits — by getting the workers to work harder. If they worked harder, the mines would produce more gold, and more gold meant more profits.

Mine-owners and their managers found different ways of making their workers more productive. For example:

Two jobs for the price of one:

There were two important underground jobs in the mines for unskilled workers. The one job was to hammer or later, drill deep holes into the rock, so that dynamite could blow it up. The second job was to shovel the blasted rock into trucks or 'trams' and push these trams to the lifts to be taken above ground. This second job was called 'lashing and tramming'.

It took strong men to do these jobs in the hot, airless tunnels underground. To save money, the mine-owners hired all underground, unskilled workers as 'hammerboys'. But at the beginning of each shift, these men had

THE WAGE COLOUR BAR

Part II of this book has shown how the mine-owner developed a powerful system of labour control. This system enabled them to create a huge black labour force and maintain it as cheaply as possible, with minimum wages.

Soon after the Chamber of Mines was formed, the mine-owner members came to an agreement not to compete for labour. They agreed that all the mining companies would pay black workers a maximum wage — not more than two shillings

and three pence (22 1/2) cents for a ten-hour shift. If any mine offered a black worker more than the maximum, the mine-owners would have to pay a fine to the Chamber. In this way, black wages were kept low, and the profits higher.

Black workers were not free to move around the towns and offer their labour for the best wages. They were forced to work under a powerful system of labour control.

It was this system of control that kept black wages so low on the mines. We can call this system the *wage colour bar.*

to do a few hours of lashing and tramming. Only after they had done this work could they start on the job that they were paid for — which was drilling.

So in each shift mine workers were doing extra work, although this was not part of the contract. In this way they did more work for the same wage — in other words, two jobs for the price of one.

The Loafer-Ticket System:

There was another way that the mine-owners pushed the workers to work harder — the loafer-ticket system. This is how the system worked.

At the end of the day's shift the driller had to show that he had drilled at least 30 inches of rock. If he drilled 30 inches or more, the supervisor gave him a ticket. When the hammer man had collected 30 tickets, he was entitled to his monthly wage.

But if a hammer man did not manage to drill the 30 inches, he would get a 'loafer's ticket' — for not working hard enough. A loafer's ticket meant that a worker got no money for that ten-hour shift: he was allowed only porridge for his lunch and supper.

The loafer-ticket system gave the mine-owners extra work for no pay. Every hammer man had to do a few hours' lashing and tramming. Then, if he was even an inch short of the 30 inches at the end of the shift, he got no pay for his work. The loafer-ticket system was very profitable for the mine-owners.

LONGER CONTRACTS

The mine-owners were anxious to keep workers on the mines for as long as possible. The longer the workers stayed, the more experienced they became and the better they worked. Profits went up, and recruiting costs stayed down.

The mine-owners used differ-

ent methods to keep workers as long as possible on the mines.

Less money to spare:

One way to keep labourers on the mines for longer was to make sure they did not get, or save, enough money to leave. The mine-owners knew very well that as migrants, black workers would go home as soon as they had saved enough money; and that they would stay at home as long as their money lasted.

Mine-owners often used this fact as a reason for paying low wages. For example one mine manager told a government commission in 1904:

'A large increase in wages will defeat its object, as the Native will work for a shorter period.'[2]

In 1925 the Native Recruiting Corporation were still telling the government that an increase in wages was a bad thing for employers:

'The main result would be that the native works for a shorter

With increasing poverty in the reserves, more and more people became displaced. They were forced to leave home and, as best they could, take the long trek to the towns and mines to look for work.

'Working for porridge.'5 If the miner did not manage to hammer out at least 30 inches of rock per shift underground, he would get no pay for that shift. Instead, he received a 'loafer's ticket', which meant he was allowed only his meal of porridge for the day.

period than at present.'4

Mine-owners convinced the government that a low wage for black workers was necessary, or else the mines would lose their workers. Low wages forced migrant workers to work for a longer time on the mines.

Less money saved:

Mine-owners also encouraged mine-owners to *spend* their money. Trading stores were set up near the compounds.

These stores sold a wide variety of goods. They sold meat and other food for workers who were still hungry at the end of a hard day's work. They sold the boots which every worker had to buy for his work. They sold the everyday things to make life in the compound a little easier — soap, cigarettes, blankets, clothes, cards, musical instruments. They sold drink, too, until alcohol was banned to Africans in 1901.

The trading store was usually the only store near enough to the mine-worker. He was therefore forced to buy his goods there, usually at higher prices than the prices in town.

The trading stores benefited two groups of people:
1. the store-keepers made good profits from their customers;
2. the mine-owners kept their workers for a longer time. The more money the workers spent while they were working on the mines, the less money they would save.

Many workers stayed working on the mines after their contracts were finished, because they had

not saved enough money to take home.

EXTENDED CONTRACTS

By about 1910, most South African black mine-workers were being hired under six-month contracts. 'Foreigners' had to work for 12-month contracts.

But these contracts took longer than six and twelve months to complete. Most workers found that they were working for seven or 14 months. In other words, their contracts were *extended.* How did this happen?

* Firstly, the Chamber of Mines laid down that 30 shifts must be counted as a month of work. In other words, a worker had to work 30 shifts before he could get his monthly wage. But it took longer than a month to finish 30 shifts because workers had to have days of rest occasionally.

So mine labourers had to work over a period of 34 or 35 days to work off one month of their contract.

In this way, mine-labourers were paid only for their labour, not for their days of rest. At the same time, the mine-owners got longer contracts, and more work, from each worker.

* There was another way the contracts were extended. As we have seen, each worker had to 'earn' 30 tickets before he collected his monthly wage. When a worker got a loafer's ticket he lost a day's work. A loafer's ticket extended his contract by yet another day. So, for example, if a worker got 12 loafer's tickets during his contract on the mines, he would have to stay on and work for an extra 12 shifts before he com-

pleted his contract.

The loafer ticket system was 'a double punishment', said one mineworker to a government commission in 1913. 'They do not get their tickets marked and they are not paid for that day and the contract is not going on.[6]

The system of 30 shifts a month therefore combined with the loafer ticket system to keep the workers for weeks, or even months longer than they expected.

A SYSTEM OF FORCED LABOUR

As the years went by, more and more migrant workers were working for longer periods on mines. Most Mozambique workers were staying for nearly 20 months.

Workers were staying for longer periods because the reserves were getting poorer and the cost of living was going up. Yet the wages did not go up correspondingly — on the contrary, they went down.

In 1895, for example, the average wage for the unskilled worker on the gold mines was more than R6,35 a month.

Ten years later, the unskilled worker's wage had dropped to R5,20[7]

Yet we know that there was a continuous shortage of labour in the mines. Usually when labour is short, workers' wages go up. But in the South African gold mines, wages went down in the first ten years and remained the same for the next 40 years, even though the cost of living rose higher and higher through two world wars.

Meantime, migrant workers were forced to leave home and work for longer and longer periods to save the money they needed to support their families. As they entered the wage market on the mines, they became part of a system designed to keep the wages down — the migrant labour system, the pass laws, the compound and contract systems and WNLA's methods of recruitment all added up to the wage colour bar — and served the need for profits from the gold mines.

In addition, the system of exploitation in the mines managed to squeeze even more work from unskilled workers, without extra pay.

Black workers were caught in the grip of a powerful system of labour control; so powerful that it became, in the words of the mine-owners themselves, a system of *forced labour*.

THE POWER OF THE MINE-OWNERS

The mining companies had become so powerful and important that they controlled the labour system in southern Africa, and even beyond. How did they do this?

One answer lies in the *power of the mine-owners.*
* They had power through the vast amounts of capital which they controlled.
* They had power through their 'union', the Chamber of Mines.
* And, after the Anglo-Boer War, they had power through the support of the government.

The Anglo-Boer War marks the turning point in the history of the mine-owners. After the war, from 1902, the needs of the mines dominated the country as a whole and changed the political and economic set-up of South Africa.

The next two pages deal with the Anglo-Boer War and its significance to the mine-owners.

THE HUNGRY MINES

'Roughly speaking, more whites meant less profits and more natives meant more profits... The appetite of the mining industry for native labour was therefore great.'
— Franklin, *Economics in SA*

THE MINE-OWNERS SAID:

'They should compel the native to contribute his quota to the good of the community ... to work.'

— *J. Rudd, 1899*[9]

'With good government there will be an abundance of labour, and with an abundance of labour there will be no difficulty in cutting down wages.'
— *Hayes-Hammond, 1899*[10]

'The less he is paid, the longer he remains, and the more efficient he becomes.'
— *Sir Lionel Phillips, 1893*[11]

The Anglo—Boer War

In 1899 the British went to war against the Boers. The war was fought for the control of the Transvaal. Gold was an important cause. The British believed that whoever controlled the Rand would control the rest of South Africa. They won the war, but it took them three years to defeat the Boers.

THE BRITISH

By the end of the 19th century, Britain governed countries all over the world. These *British colonies* made up the *British Empire.* The Cape and Natal were both British colonies in South Africa.

When gold was discovered in the Transvaal, the British government was worried that this small republic would draw the capital and the labour of the Cape and Natal away from the Empire.

Most of the Randlords supported Britain. They were angry with the Transvaal government because the mines were being taxed to develop the interests of the Boers. They felt they would be better off governed by a modern capitalist state like Britain. The capital for the gold mines came mostly from Britain and Europe, anyway.

For these reasons the Randlords were happy to see the British win the war.

Above: British artillery men.
Below: The British army marching to war.
Inset: British soldiers killed at the battle of Spioenkop.

And the Mines 1899—1902

Three generations of Boer 'freedom fighters'.

A Boer commando marching to war.

THE BOERS

The two Boer republics, the Transvaal and the Orange Free State, were ruled by white farmers.

When gold was discovered the Transvaal government was anxious to use taxes from the gold mines to develop commercial farming and factories so that the Transvaal would not have to rely only on gold.

They were anxious to build up their strength before the mine-owners became powerful enough to take over the country. The Boers were also very suspicious of the British.

The Boers had already fought the British in the Transvaal in 1881 (Die Eerste Vryheids Oorlog). In 1895 they squashed a plot to overthrow the Transvaal government. The plot was supported by mine-owners, including the rich and powerful Rhodes.

The Boers disagreed with the mine-owners on other matters too. They disagreed about labour policy, for example. The Boers wanted to use the pass system to keep labour on the farms, while the mine-owners felt that the government was not strict enough about directing labour to the mines.

President Kruger, president of the Transvaal, was unhappy about the thousands of foreigners who had come to the Rand in search of riches. He was afraid that they would soon outnumber the Boers and the Transvaal would cease to be a Boer state.

The Boers had left the Cape seventy years earlier so that they could be independent of Britain. But now it seemed that the wealth of the Transvaal would be their downfall.

British troops burn a farmhouse (above). The British regarded every Boer farmhouse as a source of food and sanctuary for the enemy and the Boer family as a nest of spies. General Roberts developed a 'scorched earth' policy — all farmhouses, wagons, crops and animals were destroyed. About 130 000 women and children were herded into concentration camps 'for their safekeeping', but over 20 000 died. (Right) a child's funeral.

The war lasted much longer than the British generals expected. They had one of the best armies in the world, but British soldiers were fighting in a country they did not know well. Their large armies moved slowly across the veld, an easy target for the Boer guerrilla fighters. The Boers knew the veld, they knew where to hide, they were good shots, and they could move quickly on their sure-footed, Basuto ponies.

The War was 'a white man's war.'

There was one thing the two sides did *not* disagree about — and that was the position of blacks in the Transvaal. Both sides wanted a large supply of well controlled, cheap labour.

Officially, neither the British nor the Boers would allow blacks to join them in fighting against the other side. Yet it is believed that as many as 100 000 blacks served in the war as scouts, spies, drivers, labourers, stretcher bearers and servants.

'By the end of the war, nearly 10 000 Africans were serving under arms in the British forces,' claims Thomas Pakenham in his book, *The Boer War*.

In Mafeking, 2 000 Africans were chased out and left to starve in the veld because of food shortage. Yet when the Boers attacked Mafeking, it was largely the Barolong who trapped them, saving the city for the British. No thanks was given to the Barolong, no compensation for their loss of lives and cattle in this 'white man's war'.

Many black farmers suffered from loss of crops, cattle theft and burnt-down homes during the war. On the Rand, black workers were trapped when the war started and the mines closed down. They could not get home. Thousands were put into concentration camps and kept there at a cost to Britain of less than a cent a day each. There were hundreds of deaths there, due to weakness and infection. In fact, there were even more deaths in the black concentration camps than there were in the concentration camps set up for the Boers — in which more than 20 000 women and children lost their lives.

Flogging an African tied to a wagon wheel — an everyday occurrence in British and Boer camps.

From the diary of Colonel B.P. Baden-Powell, during the siege of Mafeking, April 20:

'*Meat and meal stocks at present will last till June 12. But by forcing the natives away from Mafeking we can get their share of horseflesh for whites.*'

Extract of letter to Colonel Baden-Powell from Boer commander, Cronjé:

'*It is understood that you have armed the Bastards, Fingoes and Barolongs against us — in this you have committed an enormous act of wickedness . . . reconsider the matter, even if it cost you the loss of Mafeking . . . disarm your blacks and thereby act the part of a white man in a white man's war.*'[1][2]

Most educated blacks supported the British in this war. They believed that if Britain won the war they would restore land to blacks and give them rights such as the vote and freedom to move where they wished. After all, the new British Governor of the Transvaal, Lord Milner, told a group of blacks in 1901: 'It is not race or colour, but civilisation which is the test for political rights.'

But they were bitterly disappointed. Even 'civilised' blacks failed to get the vote after the war ended. Instead, the British government in the Transvaal passed a number of discriminatory laws on labour taxes, labour contracts, segregation of housing, finger printing of mine workers, as well as liquor laws and stricter pass laws. Milner even allowed the mines to use convict labour.

The 'liberal' British therefore had even greater control over Africans than the Boers had before the war, because the new government aimed to set up a modern capitalist state in the Transvaal under British rule.

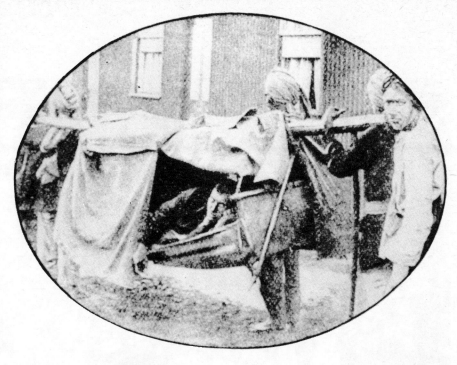

(Right) Sir Alfred Milner, the British governor of the Transvaal after the war. He was determined to transform South Africa into a modern, capitalist British state — with the help of the mines.
(Top) Nearly 1 000 Indians served in Gandhi's Ambulance Corps with the British troops, risking their lives to rescue the wounded from the battle fields and carry them to places of safety and medical attention.

Black artillery men loading a British cannon.

'It is my desire to see the strength of the state and the strength of the mining industry renovated . . . I can only compare these two, the state and the mining industry, as twins.' (Sir George Albu, Mine-owner.)[13]

The Anglo-Boer War settled the question of whose interests the mines were to serve — the Boer farmers or the new breed of capitalists who owned the mines. When Britain won the war, the mine-owners were given every assistance in building up the mines again so that the Transvaal could be transformed into a modern capitalist state. Government administration became more efficient.

After the war, there was a boom in the economy. Trade increased, there were higher profits in the stock exchange — and the wages of the workers dropped.

For the next quarter of a century, the interests of the mine-owners and their backers in Britain dominated the politics and economy of South Africa. The needs of other interest groups, the commercial farmers and the emerging factory owners, took second place in the economy.

The mining capitalists owned newspapers and journals through which they were able to influence people's thinking. It came to be accepted by those who had power that the well-being of all South Africans — including millions of black workers and their families — depended on looking after the needs of the mines.

For the next twenty years, successive governments passed laws and enforced order in the service of the mines, helping to cut down labour costs and increase mining profits.

The period after the Anglo-Boer War, therefore, saw the triumph of the mine-owners. Their interests came to dominate nearly every aspect of South African life.

PART THREE

WORKERS' RESISTANCE

In this section we shall see how workers tried to resist the control of the mine-owners over them.

Blacks were not the only workers on the mines. The mine-owners recruited far and wide to find labour to suit their needs — they imported workers from China, from the coal mines of Wales and Cornwall in Britain, and from the lesser gold mines in America and Australia.

The treatment and conditions of these workers varied immensely, but they all had one thing in common — all were wage-earners, labouring to make profits for the gold mines. And when they were dissatisfied with their employers, they expressed their resistance in whatever way they could.

In this section we shall first examine the conditions of the Chinese mineworkers. We begin with the background to the coming of the Chinese, their conditions of work and resistance to these conditions.

We shall also look at the coming of the white, skilled miners to the Rand, how their work changed, and their relationship with the mine-owners.

Lastly, we shall deal with the ways in which black workers, seriously weakened by a forced labour system, defended themselves.

Chapter Thirteen

Black Workers Boycott the Mines

The Anglo-Boer War ended with the defeat of the Boers in 1901. During the fighting, the mine-owners closed down the mines and went on 'holiday' to the Cape until the war was over. In 1901, when the British entered the Transvaal, the mines started up again. Most of the mine-owners were very pleased with the result of the war, because the new British government in the Transvaal did a lot more to help the mines than the old Boer government. For a start, it introduced stricter laws to control labour.

In 1902 the mine-owners dropped the wages of black unskilled workers. They announced that the new wages would be 30 shillings to 35 shillings a month (which was about 15 shillings or R1,50 less than workers were getting before the war.) The mine-owners were confident that with the new government's tighter control of the labour force, workers would have to accept jobs on the mines at lower wages.

But the mine-owners were wrong. Many black labourers did not return to the mines after the war. They stayed home, or they went elsewhere for jobs.

After the war there was a lot of rebuilding in South Africa. The Cape and Natal both started building new railway lines. The ports became busy again and needed more labourers too. The de Beers Dynamite factory and the diamond fields in Kimberley were also looking for more workers. They went to these places and not back to the gold mines.

All of these employers were paying higher wages than the mines.

The work was not underground and it was not dangerous.

The employers did not demand long contracts, as the mine-owners did.

For all these reasons, the gold mines on the Witwatersrand were the *last* place that unskilled workers went to look for jobs.

The result — a massive shortage of cheap labour for the mine-owners.

Black workers had resisted the attempt to lower their wages by 'voting with their feet' — that is, by withdrawing their labour.

Workers load a steam trolley in the railway goods yard, Johannesburg. After the war there was a boom in the economy and many black workers found alternative employment to mine work, for higher wages.

The mine-owners now realised that the new government controls were not enough to force black workers into the mines at the low wages they were offering. But they did not raise mine-labourers' wages. Instead, they began to look for unskilled labour outside of Africa. They called for thousands of unskilled workers from China.

Some of the first Chinese workers to be brought to the Rand to ease the shortage of labour on the mines.

Chapter Fourteen
The Chinese Workers

MIGRANT WORKERS FROM ACROSS THE WORLD

In May, 1904, the first 10 000 Chinese labourers arrived to work on the Witwatersrand gold mines. They continued to come for the next four years. By 1908 the Chamber of Mines had brought nearly 100 000 workers to the gold mines. Then they were sent back to China.

How and why did the Chinese come to work on the mines? Why did they not stay on? These questions are discussed in this chapter.

British agents on a Chinese dhow, *or boat, recruiting for the Rand gold mines.*

In their search for cheap labour, why did the mining companies look towards China?

At that time, there were thousands of unemployed in that country. During the 19th century, the great Chinese Empire had become weak and divided. The new industrial countries of Western Europe moved in and weakened the old empire even further. Europeans gradually took over control of the trade. China became poorer and poorer. Her riches were leaving the country in European ships and she was getting very little in return. To make things worse, there was a war between Russia and Japan over north China. Refugees streamed into the towns.

Millions were left without employment and became desperate — they would take any jobs they could get. The mine-owners in South Africa knew this and they knew that Britain had control over parts of China. So they

This copy of a 1907 British Tory Party election poster (below) defends the Chinese labour policy on the Rand.

DON'T WORRY, THE CHINAMAN WON'T SNEAK YOUR BUSINESS, MR. TRADER; HE CAN'T BUY YOUR LAND, MR. FARMER; HE CAN'T GET YOUR JOB, MR. SKILLED WORKMAN.

began to organise a recruiting system to bring Chinese labourers to the gold mines. At last, they felt, they had found a solution to their problem — the shortage of cheap labour.

OPPOSITION TO CHINESE LABOUR

Many groups in Britain and South Africa were against the idea of bringing Chinese labour to the Witwatersrand. They opposed it for different reasons:
* The white miners were worried that the Chinese would take over their jobs at lower wages.
* The traders were worried that the Chinese would not spend their money in the stores, but send all of it back home to their families.
* Many whites did not want any more 'people of colour' to come into the country. White newspapers began to write about the

'Yellow Peril', warning that the Chinese would stay on, grow in numbers and 'take over the country'.
* Most of the Boers were angry too. The British had won the war and the British capitalists controlled the mines. Now they wanted to bring 'non-whites' into the country just because they needed their labour. The old Transvaal Republic, they reasoned, would never have allowed Chinese into their country. The coming of the Chinese was another rude reminder to the Boers that they had lost the war.
* The Liberal Party in Britain was also against the introduction of Chinese labour on the grounds that these workers would be badly treated and underpaid.

But the mining companies were strong enough to win the argument. They promised that everyone would benefit from Chinese labour. *'In agreeing to import the Chinaman here, we were really the best friends the*

DOWN WITH CHINESE SLAVERY

A Chinese cartoon protests against the 'slave' labour and high death rate of indentured mine-workers on the Rand.

skilled artisans of this country ever had,' said the President of the Chamber of Mines to a meeting of white miners.[1]

The mines would start producing more gold, they said, if the Chinese came. This would mean more jobs for whites, and more money. Traders would do well because people would have more money to spend. The mine-owners claimed that the whole Rand would prosper as a result of Chinese labour on the mines.

They promised to bring the Chinese to the Rand under strict conditions.

CONDITIONS OF CHINESE LABOUR ON THE MINES

The Transvaal government helped to ease the fears of the white miners by listing 44 jobs which were reserved for whites only. The Chinese were not allowed to do any skilled labour, buy land, trade, or pay rent for land.

The first Chinese arrived in 1904. They came under three to four-year contracts. Their con-

tracts stated that they would have to live in the mine compounds for as long as their contracts lasted. They also had to agree to work at special, low rates of pay for at least six months to pay back the costs of recruiting and transport all the way from China.

COMPOUNDS

How did the Chinese live during their stay on the gold mines?

The British government made the mine-owners build special new compounds for them. These compounds were cleaner and less crowded than the old buildings where African workers lived. (In Chapter 11 we dealt with the compound system in more detail.)

But if the workers wanted to go further than the property of the mine, like African workers, they had to get a pass.

In the beginning, the compounds seemed to work well. Chinese cooks were specially employed to cook Chinese meals, and on the whole their food was better than the food given to

African workers.

Mine managers noted that more than 92 out of every 100 workers reported for work each day. (Before the war, only 70 out of every 100 African workers were reporting every day.) Within 12 months more than 50 000 Chinese were working on the gold mines, and they all lived in compounds.[2]

Compound bunks built for the Chinese workers were small and narrow. In later years, after they left, black miners had to squeeze into these tight spaces. Crown Mines Compound.

The Chinese compound police were very important to management. They could communicate with the workers — the managers could not speak Chinese — and kept control over them.

LANGUAGE PROBLEMS

The Chinese workers could not speak English, or any other language spoken in South Africa. Yet compound managers did not learn Chinese. They relied on the Chinese 'compound policemen' to control the teams of workers.

These compound policemen were usually hard men, mostly ex-soldiers. They often treated workers badly and tricked them into giving them money in return for favours. They were often drug-sellers and dealers in gambling, which gave them more power over the workers.

Underground, the problem of language was worse. The white miners could not explain the work properly to the labourers. Instead, they used to hit and kick the workers 'to make them understand.'

The Chinese understood one thing very well: they did not like being beaten. They began to hit back. Bad feeling grew underground and the white miners began to be frightened of the Chinese.

SPARE TIME

There was no family life in the compounds. The contracts of the Chinese workers were long and their families were thousands of miles away. They were far from home, lonely and in strange surroundings. They found little friendliness from any other group. They were kept separate from other skilled workers except for some sport and drill-ing competitions against African workers.

The only women most of the Chinese workers ever saw were women of the streets. The compound hospitals had to treat most of the workers for syphilis, which they caught from prostitutes.

Gambling was another way to pass the time. It was popular because workers had a chance to increase their money. But of course, many of the men lost a lot of their money and had to stay on longer in the mines working to pay off their gambling debts.

Gambling between the dumps of a mine. In the enclosed world of the compound, recreation was limited.

A Chinese worker's sketch of a tug-of-war contest between black and Chinese miners.

66

The Chinese Workers' Resistance

DESERTION

During their first year on the Rand, more than half the Chinese workers left the mines and compounds. Some left for a few days. Others never returned.

Chinese workers deserted for the same reasons as African workers — because they were unhappy with their wages and with their working conditions. There seemed to be no other way that they could protest against working conditions. The government had banned all forms of protest by Chinese workers in 1905. Even peaceful meetings were not allowed.

However, deserting was a much more serious step for Chinese workers to take than it was for African workers. The Chinese had nowhere to go. Home was out of reach, thousands of miles across the sea. A Chinese worker had only two alternatives: either he could go back to the mines and accept the punishment for breaking his contract, or he could join a gang of other deserters and live in the veld, stealing chickens from farms or attacking white houses or stores for food.

These gangs led hard and desperate lives. Much of the time they were half starved. Sometimes they were driven to violence. In August 1905, A Bronkhorst farmer was murdered, and two months later a man was murdered near Boksburg. The white population on the Rand and some of the newspapers began to call for the Chinese to go.

But the Chinese were too useful to the mine-owners. They refused to stop employing Chinese mineworkers.

They pointed out that the Chinese did not commit more crimes than other population groups on the Rand.' Nevertheless, the mine-owners promised that they would try harder to catch all deserters, and the government gave permission to

Numbered and finger-printed, Chinese labourers pose with compound policemen and supervisors.

all whites to arrest any Chinese they saw outside the Rand.

WORKER UNREST

It was obvious that many of the Chinese workers were not happy on the mines.

About six months after the Chinese arrived, unrest began. There was trouble in a number of mines. In one mine there was a riot and a white miner was killed. In another mine, 50 leaders were arrested for refusing to obey orders. By early 1905, the managers of 77 different mines had called in the police to make the workers go back to their work.

In most cases, the workers said they were dissatisfied with their wages. They claimed that the manager had cheated them of their wages.

Before the Chinese started to work on the mines, they agreed to a contract with the management. The contract stated that for the first six months the workers would be paid a shilling a day for every ten-hour shift. Wages were so low partly because the mine-owners had spent a lot of money to import them all the way from China. The Chinese had to accept this.

The contract said that after six months, if most of the workers were earning 50 shillings for every 30 shifts, (through overtime and extra drilling) the mines would raise everybody's wages to 50 shillings. But in many mines, this did not happen. Here is one story of how the Chinese protested against the way their employers broke the contract.

A STORY OF RESISTANCE: THE NORTH RANDFONTEIN STRIKE

There were about 1 300 Chinese workers in the North Randfontein Mine. When their wages did not go up after six months, the workers chose 53 leaders to speak to the manager about their contract. These leaders politely asked for a meeting with the mine manager.

They told the manager that all the workers were expecting to be paid one shilling and sixpence a day. They had been working at the mine for more than six months, and the contract stated that their wage should be increased. The manager explained that the contract said that *most* of the workers should be earning one shilling and sixpence a day after six months. He said that *most* of the workers did not mean *all* of the workers. Nevertheless, the manager promised to talk to the government about the contract and let them know his decision later.

A week later, the manager called a meeting of all the headmen — or 'boss boys' as they were called. He offered them special bonuses if their teams worked well. This meant that the headmen would get more money, but the ordinary workers would not.

The Chinese headmen refused this offer because they did not want to be divided from the other workers. They resigned as headmen and asked to be employed as ordinary hammer men.

But the manager refused to allow the headmen to resign. He threatened them with arrest for breaking their contracts. The workers then decided to try a different method of protest — one that would not break the contract.

GO-SLOW STRIKE

According to the contract, hammer-men had to drill at least 12 inches of underground rock a day. Usually, hammer-men drilled 24 to 36 inches a day. (If they drilled more than 27 inches they would get a bonus.)

But on 29 March 1905, no Chinese hammer man at North Randfontein Mines drilled more than 13 inches of rock. They were not breaking their contract, but the mine had to stop working because there was so little ore to be crushed at the end of the shift.

This 'go slow' strike lasted for three days. Although the workers were not breaking the law, the manager called the police to arrest the leaders. The workers resisted the arrests. They sat on a mine dump, throwing bottles and sticks at the police when they tried to get up to them.

After two hours, the workers started moving towards Lancaster mine to get the workers there to join them. But the

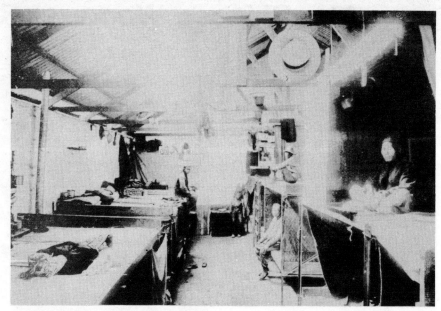
An early photograph showing the interior of a Chinese compound.

police had called more troops from Krugersdorp, and arrested the 53 leaders on their way to Lancaster mine.

The leaders were taken to court. They had not broken their contracts so they could not be charged for doing so. But they were found guilty of 'public violence', and sentenced to nine months' hard labour in jail.

RESULTS OF THE PROTEST

The Chinese workers of North Randfontein Mine lost their leaders. But the protest was not a failure. The workers had shown the managers that they were united. They had been able to co-operate in the go-slow strike without breaking any rules. They had refused to be divided — no workers had accepted the higher wages which were offered to the few. They said they wanted a 'fair wage' for everybody.

The managers had been surprised at the way the Chinese workers were united and organised during the strike. They realised that the Chinese had the power to stop the mines, and they did not want it to happen again. They therefore offered the Chinese workers these wages:
* All surface workers were to get get one shilling and sixpence a day.
* Hammer-men were offered piece work — they were to get

one shilling for every 24 inches of rock that they drilled, with a bonus for drilling more than 36 inches.

The hammer-men were satisfied with this offer. They were not afraid of hard work, but they felt strongly that they should be paid for their work.

The mine-owners and managers were also pleased. Production increased in the mines, because the hammer-men worked harder for piece rates. But the mines were not paying higher wages than before, because the slower drillers were now paid less. Piece work actually gave the managers greater control over the workers.

The North Randfontein Mine protest therefore had results for all the Chinese mine workers. Piece work for hammer-men spread to other mines on the Rand, at the same wage rates, and most of the Chinese workers became hammer-men.

Chinese mine-workers surprised their employers by showing remarkable solidarity in the North Randfontein strike.

THE CHINESE GO HOME

In 1907 the British government changed and the leader of the Liberal Party became the new Prime Minister of Britain. The Liberal Party had always been against the Chinese labour system for the Rand. Some Liberal Party supporters reported on the 'slave conditions' of the compounds, attacking the low wages the Chinese were paid and the large profits that the mine-owners were making.

After 1907, the new British government began to urge the Transvaal government to send the Chinese workers home.

Also, many whites in the Transvaal continued to oppose Chinese labour. White miners were afraid of the Chinese underground and afraid that they would take over their jobs. The public were afraid of the Chinese deserters who roamed the veld, even though there were very few of them. The Boers especially wanted them out of South Africa.

The Transvaal government wanted to please their white voters — after all, the voters could change the government in the next elections if they were not satisfied. So the government decided that the Chinese must go.

By this time, the mine-owners were prepared to send the Chinese workers home. The labour shortage was easing because more and more Africans were being brought to the mines by the WNLA recruiting system. What is more, African workers were getting lower wages than they had been getting five years earlier.

So the mine-owners started to send Chinese workers home when their contracts expired. By 1910, the last of them had left.

Altogether, about 80 000 Chinese workers came to work on the gold mines of the Rand. Three thousand men had died in accidents, suicides or from diseases. Of those who survived, only 20 men did not get home. Nobody knows how they disappeared. Some deserters may have died in caves, or in the veld. It is impossible to say.

At the end of the long contract, the Chinese workers go home. By the time they left, in 1910, the black boycott of the mines had been broken.

The South African Chinese Today

The Chinese migrant labourers came and went. They were not connected with the Chinese traders and fortune seekers who came to South Africa earlier and later, at their own expense. Chinese immigrants came mostly from the south of China, and they settled in the eastern Cape as well as in the Transvaal. As years went by, more and more South African Chinese became educated and middle-class.

They were a different class of people from the mine-workers of the Rand. Nevertheless, many whites had the same feelings about them too. They still thought of the Chinese as the 'Yellow Peril'. In fact, most whites did not like any non-Europeans to come to South Africa. They tried to stop any more Chinese from coming. In many ways, the government treated the Chinese like other blacks. They were not allowed to vote. They were not allowed to live with whites. But because their numbers were too small to bother the government, the Chinese were not separated completely from whites. The government allowed their children to go to private church schools for example, with white children; and as the years went by, some of the richer Chinese moved into white suburbs.

Today, the Chinese live in a sort of 'no-man's land'. In some ways the Chinese can live as whites — as long as they live quietly, without complaining too much. At the same time, they are treated as if they do not really belong to South Africa. They are neither 'black' nor 'white'.

An early photograph of a Chinese settler on the Rand.

69

Chinese workers 'lashing and tramming'. The exploitation of Chinese labour enabled mine-owners to weaken black resistance to lower wages.

'It is difficult to see how the Asiatic can ever become a menace . . . for he becomes merely a labourer without opportunity to exercise any personal preference, or being in any manner able to change his condition. The length of his stay is predetermined. His occupation is fixed. He has no rights except to return to his native land.'
— Editorial, S.A. Mines, January 1904.[3]

The Chinese came and went. Yet their short stay as mineworkers on the Rand was very important. After they left, things were not the same again on the gold mines.

What was the importance of their stay on the gold mines?

* *Firstly, Chinese labour saved the mines from a shortage of cheap labour.*

The mine-owners got cheap labour from China when many African workers did not return to the mines after the Anglo-Boer War. The longer contracts of the Chinese saved money for the mine-owners — the longer the Chinese workers stayed, the better they got to know their jobs. Their work produced more gold more quickly. Within a year or two after the Chinese arrived, many mines were producing more gold than before and their profits grew rapidly.

* *The low wages of the Chinese brought down the wages of all unskilled miners.*

By the time the Chinese started to leave in 1907 — 1908, black wages were the lowest they had been since before the war. The table on this page shows how black wages went down as more and more Chinese came to work on the mines. It also shows how Chinese wages began to increase after they were given piece-work rates as hammermen.

The longer the Chinese stayed, the more the mine-owners were able to bring down African wages. As more and more Chinese came to work on the mines, the mines were able to turn away Africans who came to look for work on the mines.

So the mine-owners were able to use the Chinese to break the shortage of cheap labour. When there was no longer a shortage, the mine-owners were able to pay lower wages to black, unskilled workers.

* *Job reservation for whites.*

White workers had been very worried that Chinese labourers might take over skilled jobs at lower wages. But the mine-owners promised that the Chinese would work as cheap labourers only. The Transvaal government helped by passing a law reserving 44 skilled jobs for whites only. This law, the *Transvaal Ordinance of 1904* was the first to reserve so many jobs for whites. After the Chinese left, the Ordinance stayed, to guard against black competition for skilled jobs. (Chapter 15 deals more fully with job reservation in the early years.) The coming of the Chinese labourers therefore established the South African system of job reservation on the mines.

Table showing average monthly wage for African and Chinese workers

	Chinese	Africans
1905 — 6	39s 9d	51s 11d
1906 — 7	41s 6d	52s 3d
1907 — 8	44s 3d	49s 1d

(The average wage of African workers declined over a period of three years.)[4]

White miners were anxious that Chinese workers would take over their jobs at lower wages. To appease them, the Transvaal government in 1904 reserved 44 skilled jobs for whites only. After the Chinese left, job reservation remained.

Chapter Fifteen
White Workers and the Colour Bar

In the history of resistance to the mine-owners' control, it is clear that the most important conflict of interests occurred between mine-owners and the ultra-exploited black workers — the story of their resistance follows this chapter. During this period, however, the most successful and most *noticeable* struggles occurred amongst the white workers.

This was because white workers had more power than the black workers and could challenge the mine-owners directly, through strikes, through political parties and through newspapers.

What actually were these workers resisting? Mainly, they were fighting against the mine-owners' continual attempts to replace 'expensive' white labour with 'cheap' black labour.

This chapter traces the development of the white labour force in the gold mines and explains why they were placed in a special position by the mine-owners. This special position shaped the forms of white worker resistance in South Africa.

THE NEED FOR SKILLED WORKERS

Deep-level mining was new to South Africa and there were few men in South Africa who had experience of mining deep under the ground. Some had experience in the diamond mines in Kimbeley but deep-level mining for gold was different from diamond mining. Besides, there were not enough experienced miners from Kimberley for the growing number of mines on the Rand. The mine-owners had to recruit skilled miners from other countries.

Where did these miners come from? Most of the skilled miners came from the mines of Britain — from Cornwall or Northumberland in England, and from the mines of Scotland and Wales. Many others came from the coal mines of Australia.

These new immigrants brought with them not only mining skills — they also brought their experience of being workers and we shall see later how important this was. They came to the Rand as full-time workers, with no land to go back to. The skilled miners of the early years had a strong influence on the working conditions of white workers in the years to come.

HIGH WAGES

Skilled miners in South Africa got high wages. In 1897, for example, skilled miners earned 18 pounds to 22 pounds a month. That was good pay in those days.

Unskilled miners were earning only two to three pounds a month.

There were two main reasons why skilled miners got high wages in those early years:
- their skills were in short supply;
- they had strong trade unions.

(1) *Shortage of skills* — One reason for their high wages was that the mines desperately needed skilled workers, as we have seen. So, from the earliest days, mine-owners offered high wages for skills, and skilled miners were in a strong position.

(2) *Strong Unions* — Most of these miners saw themselves as members of the working class. They organised themselves into unions soon after they arrived. They had experience of trade unions in the countries that they came from, and they knew how to bargain for higher wages and better working conditions.

In 1881 the carpenters and joiners on the Rand organised themselves into a union. In 1886 the engineering union was started. Other unions followed.

These early unions were all *craft unions* — only skilled workers qualified in a craft were allowed to join. The most important unions were the Engineering Union, with 3 000 members by 1913, and the Transvaal Miners'

Skilled miners were extremely important to the mines. In the first twenty years of deep-level mining most were recruited mainly from Britain and Australia — at high wages.

White miners at the shaft-head. To protect their jobs, the skilled miners reorganised themselves. They changed their old craft unions to industrial unions, to allow all white workers to join. Black mine-workers were excluded from these unions.

Association, with 6 000 members in 1913.

These unions became strong. The skilled miners knew how important the gold mines were to South Africa — and how important their skills were to the gold mines. They were in a good bargaining position.

In 1897, for example, the white miners at Randfontein went on strike. The manager had dropped the wage of the black miners and he tried to do the same to the white miners. The strike spread to the other mines, with the support of all the unions. The mining companies then announced that they would not drop the wages of the skilled workers.

This was the first strike on the Rand by the skilled workers, and they won it with very little trouble, that first time. The unions were able to fix skilled wages at more than one pound a day more for skilled workers. Within 15 years the unions had bargained for paid holidays, compensation for accidents and phthisis, overtime rates and shorter working hours.

But things began to change for skilled workers. As the years went by, other workers began to learn the skills of deep-level mining. The mine-owners saw that they did not need the skilled miners as much as before. The skilled workers began to lose their strong position as the mine-owners gradually gave more and more of the skilled work to blacks — at the old rates of 15 to 20 cents a day. Or else they gave jobs to semi-skilled whites with some experience, for lower pay than the skilled whites were getting. Of course the skilled miners were very worried about losing their jobs. They took action to protect themselves against the mine-owners' attack on their bargaining power and on their wages.

SKILLED MINERS FIGHT BACK

The skilled miners defended their position in various ways.
* Firstly, they opened up their unions to all white miners. The old craft unions changed to *industrial unions.* Any white miner could join the industrial union. He did not have to have a blasting certificate to become a member. In other words, the skilled miners decided to make themselves stronger by trying to unite all the white miners under one big organisation.

This was the turning point in the policy of the skilled miners. Previously, they had used their *skill* to unite them and give them strength. Now they were beginning to turn towards *race* to protect their workers' rights.
* Secondly, they began to support *political parties.* The South African Labour Party and the Afrikaner National Party tried to persuade the government to make laws to protect white workers. White workers voted for these parties.

The shift from skill to race as a unifying force for workers led to a particular viewpoint in political outlook. The white workers saw these two parties as defending their position of racial superiority in the labour market.

White miners used these two weapons — their unions and their political power — to protect themselves against the mine-owners' attempts to undermine their special position. They found that they were caught in a trap. White miners were a privileged group of workers, commanding good wages for special jobs — but their very privileges put their jobs in danger, for the mine-owners preferred to employ the cheap labour of blacks as far as possible.

The white miners resisted the mine-owners' attempts to replace them by calling for *job reservation*.

JOB RESERVATION

What exactly is job reservation? Job reservation, or the *job colour bar*, reserves certain jobs for whites only.

The job colour bar goes back a long way in South Africa. Nearly 300 years ago, slaves were brought to the Cape to do hard labour on the farms, while their white masters supervised them. In later years, when there was a struggle for land, many blacks lost their land to the Boers and British. Blacks became farm labourers for white land owners. Once again, the work was divided racially — labourers were mostly black, bosses were white.

When the diamond and gold fields started in Kimberley and on the Rand, once again blacks did most of the hard, labouring work. The first job colour bar law on the Rand was made in 1893. Although intended as a safety regulation to prevent accidents it made the assumption that blacks would never be skilled workers. The law said that engine drivers had to have certificates to show that they were skilled. It also added that no black person could hold this certificate. In other words, Africans could not become qualified engine drivers.

In the next few years more job colour bars were made. But in those first years in the mines, there were very few skilled blacks.

UNSKILLED WHITES

Then came the Anglo-Boer War, and the gold mines closed down for two years. After the war there was a shortage of cheap labour. This was partly because the mine-owners tried to drop the wages of black workers. Thousands of men stayed away from the mines.

Mine-owners then tried using unskilled white labour, but the skilled miners were against this plan. They were worried that these unskilled whites would not be properly trained and that they would take over the skilled jobs at lower wages. Then the mine-owners could lower the wages of all skilled miners.

In September 1902, about 100 skilled miners went on strike at the Village Main Reef Mine. They struck because they feared they would be replaced by unskilled white workers. The skilled miners' union, the Transvaal Miners' association, supported the strike.

(An interesting point to remember about this strike, is that the skilled miners were worried about *all* unskilled workers who might take their places. Workers of any colour who could work for lower wages could eventually take the place of the skilled workers. So skilled miners were against *white* cheap labour as well as *black* cheap labour.)

'THE YELLOW PERIL'

The Chamber of Mines then decided to import Chinese labour. You will remember that the white miners were against this plan as well. They said that the Chinese were 'devilishly clever' and would learn many of the

Impressions of an Immigrant Mine Worker

His first day at work brought startling revelations with it. The head of the workshop, Jock Davidson, handed out his tools: 'Here's your hammer,' he said, 'and here's your chisel, shifting spanner, pliers . . . and here's a nigger.'

Andrews was taken aback. 'What's he for?' he asked.

'To carry your tools,' Davidson replied tersely, and dismissed the new hand.

A few years later at Randfontein, his helper was a strong young Zulu, who asked him how much he drew in wages.

'A pound a shift,' Andrews replied.

'And how much do I get?' asked the Zulu.

'What's it — two bob a day?'

'Yes. And is that right?' the Zulu wanted to know. 'Who does all the hard work, who lifts the iron into the machine, who carries your tools for you, and hands you your tools? I do.'

As far as he was able in kitchen Zulu, Andrews put forward the argument that he got the pay of his trade because he was trained to do it. Although his 'boy' did all the heavy work, only the trained man could finish the job because of his acquired skill.

But all these arguments were unavailing. The Zulu shook his head vigorously and remained absolutely convinced on the injustice of the position . . . Andrews was deeply impressed by such incidents and turned them over frequently in his mind.

Extracts from *Comrade Bill — The Life and Times of W.H. Andrews, Workers' Leader.*
by R.K. Cope

White miners at the drill, assisted by a 'faceless' black worker.

A protest meeting, held at Boksburg, against the decision of the British government to allow Rand mine-owners to import Chinese labour. The mine-owners were able to break the 1907 strike with the help of Chinese and Afrikaner labour.

mining skills just by watching the skilled miners. Soon, they would take over the skilled jobs at 'slave wages', the white miners thought.

There were many meetings and demonstrations to protest against the coming of the Chinese. The newspapers at the time were full of discussions of the 'Chinese Question'. Mine-owners wrote articles in the papers, explaining that white miners did not need to worry. The Chinese would only do the unskilled work on the mines. But the miners did not trust the mine-owners.

'Unskilled . . . that is what they ask,' said one skilled miner. 'But how long will they consider certain work as skilled? Only as long as it takes John Chinaman to learn it — say for instance running a rock drill or sharpening drills for these machines. John Chinaman is clever and the best imitator born in this troublous world.'[1]

The skilled miners realised that already they had 'lost' some of their skills to black labourers, and they feared that they would lose even more to the Chinese.

There were many objections to the Chinese from other groups too, as we saw in the last chapter. Eventually the Transvaal government passed the *Labour Importation Ordinance* for the sake of the skilled white miners. The Chinese were to be em-

ployed *'only on such labour as is usually performed in mines in the Witwatersrand district by persons belonging to the aboriginal races or tribes of Africa south of the Equator,'* said the Ordi-

nance.[2]

In other words, the Chinese were allowed to compete with black labour only, and not with expensive, skilled white labour — for the time being.

The 1907 Strike

In 1907 there was another re-organisation of the work to save more costs for the mines. The mine-owners instructed the white miners to supervise three drills instead of two. This led to another strike. Within three weeks, more than 4 000 miners were on strike on the Rand. But the mine-owners were prepared. With the help of the government, they sent out notices to all unemployed Afrikaners to go down to the mines and take the place of the British workers. The unemployed

were desperate for jobs. They did not really understand the skilled miners' complaints. The strikers picketed the mines — they stood outside the mines and told workers not to go down.

'Timbermen! Let the scabs protect themselves! Boilermakers! Leave holes in the boilers!' urged a pamphlet.[3]

But the government called out the army. The army beat up the strikers and protected those who went to work. The strike was broken. Unskilled Afrikaners and

Members of a craft union on an outing, with their two black retainers.

74

experienced Chinese kept the mines going. Slowly, the skilled miners went back to work. But ten percent of the miners lost their jobs, and the mines saved a quarter of the costs of breaking rock with the new system.

After the strike, the Transvaal government appointed a commission to listen to the complaints of both sides. The commission interviewed mine-owners, managers and white workers to hear their opinions. It was quite obvious that mine-owners and managers felt that they no longer needed the skilled miners as much as before. They made it clear that they wanted more black labour in the mines and less white labour.

The manager of Geldenhuis Estate Gold Mining Company, for example, told the Commission:

'We have some of the Kaffirs who are better machine-men than some of the white men. I have boys who have been working on the mine from twelve to fifteen years, and they are better than many on the Rand nowadays.'
Question: *'Can they place holes?'*
Answer: *'Yes, they can place the holes, fix up the machine and do everything that a white man can do, but, of course, we are not allowed to let them blast.'*
Question: *'If the law was not what it is, do you think they could blast with safety?'*
Answer: *'I do not think; I feel sure about it. I have had experience with natives since 1879, and I know what a native can do.'*[4]

Another manager said: *'The trouble with the mines is that underground the white labour so-called is not labour at all; it is merely supervision... We have far too many whites employed on the mines. In my opinion two men are employed underground doing work one man could do easily. The white man underground is not a working man at all; he has not to work as in other countries where there is no large supply of unskilled coloured labour.'*[5]

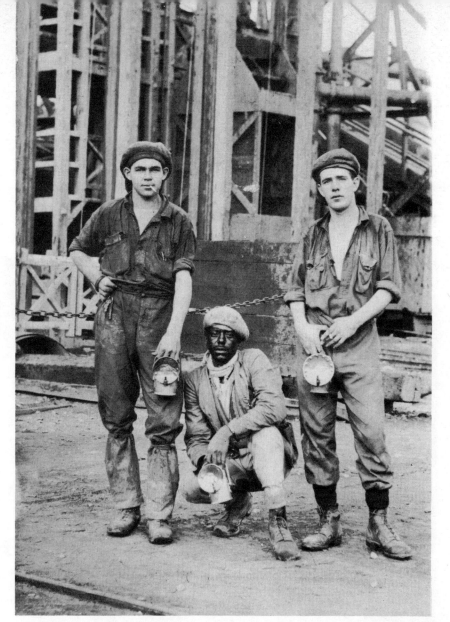

Inexperienced Afrikaners learnt a great deal from black miners 'on the job', both during and after the 1907 strike.

And a mine-owner, Sir George Albu, wrote in the *Mining Review* at the time of the strike:

'Why not make the Native the real miner... and thus save much of the money paid to White men for work they never perform?'[6]

This kind of talk worried the white miners. It seemed to them that in order to fight the mine-owners they would also have to fight the black workers. They saw black workers as 'the tools of Capitalism against the white workers'[7]. But to keep their privileged position they would have to unite all the white miners in one strong organisation. They would also have to try to build up their political power.

POLITICAL ORGANISATION

The white miners were able to defend their position with a weapon denied to black workers — they had the vote.

After the 1907 strike, many miners began to show a greater interest in politics. Most of them had had the vote since the British won the Anglo-Boer War. Many white miners hoped that their voting power would help their position at work. But the white workers were not all united in their ideas of what they wanted. Some saw themselves as mainly British, others as Afrikaners first. Many white workers did not regard themselves as workers at all.

Hundreds of workers voted for the governing *Het Volk* party. Later, when the Afrikaner National Party was formed, most

Afrikaner workers voted for it.

But many white workers supported the new Labour Party, which wanted to represent the white workers.

THE LABOUR PARTY

In the 1910 elections, the South African Labour Party managed to get four of its members into parliament. The Labour Party aimed to make the government pass laws to protect the white workers
* from employers;
* from the competition of cheap black labour.

The South African Labour Party was a white workers' party. Their members talked about a 'civilised labour' policy. This really meant jobs for whites only. It is interesting to note that the Labour Party had a kind of apartheid policy before the Afrikaner National Party developed it. They argued that South Africa should be divided into different areas for the different races.

Above: White miners outside a boarding house.
Above left: There were very few white women in Johannesburg's early years.
Left: An all-male picnic on a day off.

After the Anglo-Boer War, mining companies built houses to accommodate their white staff. White miners were fortunate in being able to settle in the towns with their families.

They believed that:
* Blacks should be left alone to farm on the reserves. They did not really need wages. The mine-owners were forcing them to leave home to go to work.
* All the immigrant 'Asiatics' should be sent back to India. They should not be allowed into South Africa.
* 'Coloureds' would gradually disappear if mixing of the races was prevented. 'Coloureds' would then become part of the black race and live separately from the whites.

With this policy, the Labour Party hoped to keep all mining and factory jobs in the towns for whites only. Then white wages would not drop, they hoped.

The Labour Party turned out to be mainly a party for some of the English-speaking workers, plus a few dissatisfied lawyers, teachers and shopkeepers. They had no direct power to change laws to help white workers, because they had so few members in parliament.

Nevertheless, the governing party realised that many white workers had voting power, and the government tried to satisfy some of the needs of the white worker.

THE 1911 MINES AND WORKS ACT

In 1911 the government passed a law to protect white workers. The Labour Party supported this law, although they complained that it did not go far enough to protect white workers against cheap black labour.

The Mines and Works Act set aside 32 types of jobs in the Transvaal and the OFS for whites. No blacks could qualify for certificates in these jobs. The law prevented thousands of blacks, especially 'coloureds' from getting skilled wages as engine drivers, carpenters, blasters and other skilled positions in the mines. The Mines and Works Act was the first job colour bar law in the newly formed Union of South Africa.

Nevertheless, the Mines and Works Act did not stop more and more skilled jobs going to blacks in the mines — but at black wage rates. For example:

In 1907, the Chamber of Mines employed 2 234 white miners to supervise 1890 machines.
In 1913 the mines were employing 2 207 white miners to supervise 4 781 rock drill machines.[8]

These rock drills were being handled by Africans. White miners were supervising six to ten black drillers. They also had black 'boss boys' to help them. In other words, the mines were employing more workers for more jobs, but these jobs were going to blacks, not whites, at cheap black wages.

At the same time, mine-owners felt that white miners were being paid too much for the work that they were doing. After all, they argued, they could get the work done much more cheaply by blacks. One mine-owner complained that the white miners 'were allowed to earn an exorbitant amount of money.'

THE 1913 STRIKE

In 1913, white miners went on strike again. The strike had a small beginning at New Kleinfontein Mine. In May of that year,

Tom Mathews (above) the militant trade unionist in action during the 1913 strike. Detested by Smuts, he was also outspoken against the mine-owners' failure to reduce silicosis underground. 'We consider that our health is to us more important than your dividends,' he challenged them. Tom Mathews died from silicosis in 1915.[10]

The Killer Silicosis

Silicosis is a disease of the lungs, caused by breathing in the tiny, sharp particles of dust created by the drills of deep-level mining. Silicosis was usually followed by other lung infections such as TB and pneumonia, leading to a quick death.

Silicosis was not generally recognised as a deadly problem until after the Anglo-Boer War. When the gold mines closed down during the war, many skilled miners returned to their homes in Britain, only to die there, coughing in agony.

After the war, mine-owners began to call for skilled miners to return from Britain. They discovered that many of these miners had died and were forced to face the problem. Prizes were offered for the best inventions to prevent silicosis, but these brought their own dangers (such as the water spray, which gave the men pneumonia) or else the mine-owners were not prepared to pay large sums for the more expensive equipment.

Silicosis became an important issue in the 1907 strike, when white miners were instructed to supervise three drills instead of two or one. This meant that the miners were exposed to more dust and the danger of silicosis was therefore greater.

It was found that the Rand rock driller could hope to live for only five years — he died at an average age of 37 years. Records show that in 1902 the mines employed 1337 white rock-drillers — in just over two years, 225 of those workers were dead.

Silicosis also attacked the blasters, the trammers and the lashers. In fact, all underground workers were in danger of getting this disease.

We do not know how many black workers died from silicosis. After their contracts, many migrant workers went home again, never to return.[9]

the New Kleinfontein mine-owners appointed a new manager to get more work out of the white miners.

The manager decided to re-organize the working hours. He ordered five underground engineers to work on a Saturday afternoon. When they refused, the management fired them and replaced them with five other miners who did not belong to the Transvaal Miners' Association, the miners' union. The union then sent one of their officials to speak to the mine manager, but the mining company refused to negotiate with the union. The miners then went on strike and the strike spread to other mines.

On the East Rand, groups of strikers marched from mine to mine urging miners to stay away from work. The strike spread to 63 mines, with more than 19 000 miners out on strike.

The mines were *picketed* — the strikers held up signs urging people to stay away from work. Some strike-breakers, or 'scabs', were even beaten up by the strikers. Armed police were sent to guard the entrances to the mines, to protect the strike-breakers.

The government claimed to be neutral in this struggle between white miners and the Chamber of Mines — they said they did not want to take sides. But as the strike spread to Johannesburg

Strike meeting in 1913.

and the West Rand, they sent 3 000 soldiers and policemen to the Rand.

On 4 July, the police and army broke up a banned meeting in Market Square in Johannesburg, beating people with batons, pick-handles and swords.

THE GOVERNMENT STEPS IN

At this point, the government decided to stop the strike. General Louis Botha the Prime Minister, and General Smuts the Minister of Defence, had a meeting with the union leaders in Johannesburg. Botha and Smuts

promised that the strikers would get their jobs back, with an eight-hour working day and no work on Saturday afternoons. They also promised that the unions would be recognised. In a few days, the miners went back to work.

But the strikers were soon disappointed. The government did not pass new laws to protect the white miners. Instead, in 1914 the government passed the *Riotous Assemblies Act*. This law gave the government the power to ban outdoor meetings. All picketing was also banned. Trade union officials could be charged if any illegal action was taken by

During the 1913 strike, the government sent 3 000 troops to the Rand. Soldiers and police used strong-arm tactics, shooting down unarmed men, women and children in a demonstration outside the Rand Club.

the trade unions. In fact, soon after the act was passed, trade union leaders were arrested and sent back to England.

So, in the end, the white miners lost the strike. They had struck for the right to bargain as a union and not just as employees of any one or other mining company — and for the right of their unions to bargain with their employers.

They realised that the power of white workers would be further eroded unless their trade unions were strong and united.

To unite the white workers against their employers, they tried to prevent scabs from working.

They wanted their trade union to be recognised, but the government had come out on the side of the mine-owners. The trade

unions lost the battle in 1913.

THE MINES AND THE FIRST WORLD WAR

In August 1914, Britain and Germany went to war. This was the start of the First World War. All of the British Empire — including South Africa — was at war against Germany, which had developed into a powerful rival in trade and colonies.

The First World War was a good time for the Chamber of Mines. The war brought a business 'boom' to Britain and Europe as factories were busy making weapons — guns, tanks, bullets and bombs, as well as other goods needed for the war. Britain needed more capital for its growing factories and banks. The

price of gold went up and the Rand mines prospered.

A 'DEAL' WITH THE UNION

In 1914, the Chamber of Mines decided to recognise the trade unions. It held meetings with the South African Mineworkers' Union and came to a number of agreements. The Chamber of Mines offered white miners bonuses, more overtime pay and paid holidays. The Chamber also agreed not to increase the number of black workers or machines that white miners had to supervise.

At first, the Chamber of Mines would only deal with each mining union separately. They came to an agreement with the mechanics' union, for example, and a

Soldiers in a trench in the First World War (1914 – 1918). A large number of English-speaking Rand miners joined the South African armed forces, leaving a shortage of white mining skills on the Rand. An important result of this shortage was the increased bargaining power of the remaining white workers.

By the Status Quo Agreement between the Chamber of Mines and the white Mineworkers' Union in 1918, the mining companies undertook not to employ black workers unless they increased the number of white workers correspondingly.

separate one with the engine drivers' union.

But after the unions refused to make any more agreements without the South African Industrial Federation, the Chamber of Mines began to include the SAIF in the discussions. From 1917, the SAIF played an important part in settling disagreements between white miners and management.

Why did the Chamber of Mines decide to recognise the white trade unions?

After all, the white miners had lost the 1913 strike and the government had passed the Riotous Assemblies Act to control strikes.

There were a number of reasons why the mine-owners wanted the co-operation of the white miners:

* Firstly, the war had caused a greater shortage of skilled labour. Most of the skilled miners were English-speaking and many of them had left to fight in the war against the Germans in Europe. The mine-owners wanted to avoid disagreements with the miners who were left in the mines — they could not afford interruptions of work through strikes or disputes. Britain was paying a good price for gold, and the mine-owners were anxious to keep the mines running smoothly.

* Secondly, the Chamber of Mines began to realise that the trade unions could be useful to the mine-owners. They realised that trade union officials did not always react in the same way as the workers did. They saw that trade union officials could sometimes be persuaded to make agreements with management when workers would be too angry to settle a quarrel with their employers.

As one manager said:

'The (trade union) official is more likely to take the business point of view and examine the situation calmly than the workman who has some personal grievance rankling in his mind.'[11]

So the mining management hoped to draw the trade unions a little closer to the employers and a little further away from the workers' point of view. They realised that they could get the unions, including the SAIF, to control the miners for them.

* There was also another important reason why the Chamber of Mines moved towards working with the trade unions — they were worried about the growing dissatisfaction of the black mineworkers.

The black workers had gone on strike in 1913 after the white

miners' strike. (The next chapter gives more details of the strike.) The mine-owners felt that strikes by white miners were having a serious effect on black workers. If all the 200 000 black workers went on strike the gold industry of South Africa would be crippled. It was important therefore to keep them strictly controlled.

So the co-operation between the Chamber of Mines and the white unions was a success for the mine-owners. There were few strikes during the war years, and even these were small and quickly stopped, with the help of the unions.

THE STATUS QUO AGREEMENT

In 1918, the First World War ended. In that same year the South African Mineworkers' Union negotiated with the Chamber of Mines to protect the jobs of the white miners. The mine-owners agreed that for every 17 black workers on the mines, they would employ two whites at skilled wages. This was called the *Status Quo Agreement.* It meant that if the mines wanted to employ more black workers, they would also have to employ more whites.

NEW LABOUR PROCESS

After the war, however, the situation began to change. The factories in Britain and Europe slowed down. The price of gold dropped to the old rates. Profits were smaller. To make matters worse the price of heavy machinery used in the mines was three times as much as it had been before the war. So the expenses of the mines went up.

Many mines were struggling to make a profit. The Chamber of Mines declared that 24 mines would close unless they could save money somehow. Mine-owners began to think of new ways of cutting down on their costs.

Mine-owners looked again at the job colour bar. They could not drop the wages of the black miners — they were so low already. But they could save another way. The Chamber of Mines announced that they were going to reorganise the work in the mines. They were going to introduce a new machine drill, called the *jack-hammer*. It could drill between 20 and 40 holes per shift, instead of the four to six of the old drill.

However, the use of this drill would make hundreds of white miners redundant. It would 'de-skill' their jobs, and the new semi-skilled jobs could then be given to experienced black miners — at the same low 'black' wages!

This new labour process would therefore mean more black and fewer white miners. It would go against the Status Quo Agreement, but the Chamber of Mines argued that if the mines could save money, they would not have to close down.

The Chamber spent many months with the SAIF bargaining for these changes. The SAIF agreed to some small changes but no more. In December 1921 the Chamber announced at last that they could not wait any longer as they were losing valuable profits. They dropped the wages of many of the white miners and laid off many more. They also declared that they would have nothing further to do with the SAIF.

These two photographs show the change in the labour process underground. Above left: In this early photograph a white miner operates the drill with a black 'helper'. Below: Years later the job has been 'deskilled' — black workers operate complex machinery at the same low wage they were getting before. It was the low wage of the black workers — the wage colour bar — that encouraged mine-owners to reorganise the work, and threatened the jobs of the white miners.

The 1922 Strike

In January 1922 the unions declared a general strike by all white miners.

In the next few weeks, about 25 000 miners stayed away from work. The strike leaders demanded a return to the old *Status Quo* job colour bar agreement of 1918 but the Chamber of Mines refused.

Strikers began to 'pull out the scabs' who were going to work. They armed themselves with guns and took over the mines. They refused to allow blacks to go down the mines to work.

The Prime Minister, General Smuts, then called in the army. Aeroplanes dropped bombs on Benoni and Germiston. There was shooting and fighting in the Johannesburg streets. After four days of armed struggle, the strikers were beaten.

One hundred and fifty-three people were killed and over 500 were wounded. Five thousand strikers were arrested and were imprisoned or fined. Four men were sentenced to death and hanged. By 16 March 1922 the mines were operating again. The white miners had lost the strike.

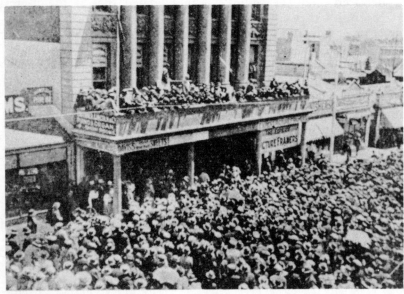

THIS PAGE: (Above left) A meeting and outside the Trades Hall in Rissik Street, on 6 March, the day a general strike was declared. (Above right) The Fordsburg police station, burnt out by strikers. (Below) Mounted police rush strikers in Rissik Street.

OPPOSITE PAGE: (Top) Sabotage — the mail train, derailed at Union Junction. There were several attempts to wreck railway lines during the strike. (Centre) The Brakpan Commando. . The strikers' access to guns enabled them to form 'strike commandos', which engaged in open battles with policemen and troops. They also used force to 'pull out the scabs' who were not on strike. (Bottom) Troops occupy the trenches in Market Square, Fordsburg. The strikers had their headquarters in Market Buildings, and held 50 policemen captive for three days.

THE RESULTS OF THE STRIKE

The white miners went back to work for a wage cut of 25 to 50 percent less than they had earned before the strike. They also lost two paid holidays. More important, many whites lost their jobs to blacks — at much lower wages. Blacks took over semi-skilled manual work such as drill-sharpening, waste-packing, engine driving, pumping and carpentry. Whites spent most of their day supervising these black workers.

The mine-owners also saved more money by allowing black workers to start the working day without their white supervisors — whites worked an eight-hour day only while blacks did a ten-hour shift. So in this way the mines saved money on white wages, while production continued.

Those were the immediate results of the 1922 strike. But the strike also had far-reaching results for the whole country.

A NEW GOVERNMENT

The white workers had lost some of their jobs and suffered a drop in wages. But they still had one weapon left — the vote. In the next elections, in 1924, the white workers and their supporters voted against the Smuts government. They felt that the Smuts government was on the side of the capitalists, the mine-owners.

A new government came to power. It was a government of two parties — the Labour Party and the Afrikaner National Party. The Labour Party got its votes from many English-speaking wage-earners, while most Afrikaner workers voted for the National Party. The Afrikaner National Party disliked the power of those 'foreign capitalists', the mine-owners. They wanted to see Afrikaner capital in its place.

The new government was called the *Pact Government*. The Pact Government promised to bring back 'law and order' to the

Prime Minister Smuts addresses the troops outside Park Station, after the revolt had been put down.

A cartoon showing Smuts about to do the dirty work of the mine-owner whose portrait hangs behind him. Mine workers were deeply suspicious of the Smuts government. They felt that it had become the tool of the mine-owners — the ruling class.

The National Party was hostile to capitalism — most capitalists were non-Afrikaners in the early 1920s. In the cartoon above industrialisation results in the evils of war and revolution, bribery, destruction, trade unions, a poisonous press and a relaxation of the job colour bar.

country and control 'communists and agitators'. At the same time the new government looked after the interests of the white workers — for example, by the Mines and Works Act of 1926:

Under this law, no Africans or 'Asians' were allowed to work in jobs that needed certificates. In addition, the Pact government introduced the 'civilised labour policy', which gave job preference to white workers.

The government thus established the job colour bar for the whole country.

JOB RESERVATION WINS

After 1924, job reservation became a part of South Africa's economy. The job colour bar was used in factories all over South Africa as well as in the mines. The Pact government realised that white workers were resisting employers mainly because they were afraid of losing their jobs to the cheap labour of the blacks. They realised that the way to stop this resistance was to make the white workers feel more secure about their better-paid jobs. As the years went by, more and more whites changed their positions from skilled and semi-skilled workers to supervisors.

Job reservation separated the white workers from the rest of the workers and brought them closer to management. As supervisors, whites played an important role for the managers — they helped to control the black workers.

So, after thirty years of resistance, the white workers won the struggle to keep their wages high and to reserve privileged jobs for themselves. In time, many white mine workers became less opposed to capitalism because they saw how they themselves were benefiting from the system.

THE REAL COLOUR BAR

'The white man has less and less of a chance if the mines obtain so much power over their blacks.' Member of Parliament, S.A. Labour Party.[12]

The resistance of white miners finally led them to demand — and obtain — job reservation.

Why did they feel threatened by black workers?

Because of the migrant labour system, the mine-owners were able to exploit black workers by paying them extremely low wages.

As we saw in Section II, the Chamber of Mines fixed the wages of black workers at a maximum of 22½ cents a shift — no African worker could get more, regardless of what work he was doing, or what skills he was using. This was the real colour bar — the *wage colour bar*, based on ultra-low wages for black workers.

As time went on, the mine-owners wished to replace 'expensive' white mine labour with the 'cheap' labour of the blacks.

The wage colour bar was created by the mine-owners, not the white workers — and it was the *wage colour bar* that led to the *job colour bar* — through which white miners chose to defend their interests, according to the colour of their skins.

THE 1922 STRIKE — BEFORE AND AFTER

	1920	1925
White and black wage costs	£17½ million	less than £14 million
Average white miner's wage	£485 per year	£375 per year
Increase in gold production	nearly 8 million oz.	nearly 9½ million oz.[13]

Afrikaner road workers. Jobs for unskilled whites were few as employers preferred black workers at low wages.

For about twenty years, English-speaking miners held the top jobs in the mines. But as time went by Afrikaners began to get jobs in the mines, too. These Afrikaners, or their fathers, had once been farmers. But thousands lost their land, like so many black farmers, and were forced to go to the towns to look for work. They became wage-earning workers, and many of them managed to join the mines. This is how it happened.

In the 19th century, the Afrikaners, or Boers as they were called, managed to get control of most of the land in the Transvaal and the OFS. The governments of the Transvaal and the Free State were Boer governments. Black farmers had to become tenants of these Boer farmers or stay in the areas that the Boers allowed the chiefs. So in the early years, there was plenty of land for the Boers. They also had lots of labour, for the black tenants had to pay for Boer 'protection' and the use of land by sending part of the family to work for the landlord.

But as time went by, things began to change:

HARDSHIP ON THE LAND

* Firstly, there was less land for the Boers as their population began to grow. Boer families were large — it was usual to have eight to ten children. When the children grew up, they wanted their own farms. The land was divided into smaller and smaller pieces, too small to farm properly.
* Droughts and cattle diseases brought great hardship to many of the smaller farmers. In 1896, for example, rinderpest killed thousands of cattle in South Africa. This disease ruined many small farmers, black as well as white. The black farmers had to go to the towns to earn wages. White farmers were luckier. Some managed to hold onto their land by borrowing money — at least they owned the land that they farmed. This land was their surety if they could not pay back the loan. But many could not survive the great loss of their stock. They sold their land to richer farmers and became their tenants. These tenants, or squatters, were called *bywoners*. By the time minerals were discovered, there were many white squatters on the richer Boer farms.

Boer families were large. As the land became too small to farm productively, thousands of Boers were forced to leave the land and seek jobs in the towns.

COMMERCIAL FARMING

* The discovery of minerals made things worse for many *bywoners*. The diamond and gold mines brought industrialisation to the Rand. In 15 years, Johannesburg changed from a bare piece of veld to a city of 100 000 people. These people had to be fed. The Rand began to need commercial farming to supply its people with food. Chapter 6 on the 1913 Land Act describes how industrialisation brought more power to the Boer farmers with the most land. These rich Boers started to use more and more of their land to grow crops to sell. Many of them raised the rents of the bywoners, or asked them to leave. Hundreds of families left the land and started other jobs. Some became transport riders, taking fresh food to the towns by ox-wagon. Others became wood cutters to supply the towns with fuel.
* The Anglo-Boer War destroyed most of the *bywoners* who were left on the farms. As you know, the British burnt the farmhouses in the Transvaal and put Boer families into concentration camps. After the war, about 10 000 Boers had no land to go back to. They had to move to the towns, mostly on the Rand, to look for work.

became Workers

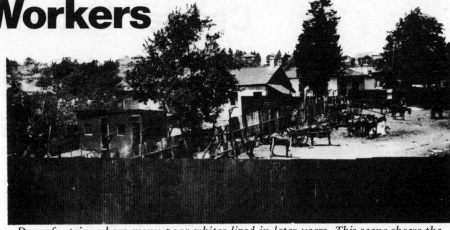

Doornfontein, where many poor whites lived in later years. This scene shows the influence of the transport services, which many Afrikaners provided before railway and motor transport became common.

Poor white children queue up for free soup, 1908. According to a government report, a quarter of school-age white children were deprived of education because of poverty.

'POOR WHITES'

Soon the towns were crowded with poor, hungry white families. Most of the men had no skills suitable to an industrial life. Even the ox-wagon drivers found that they were no longer needed — the railways had taken their place. They could not be employed as skilled miners either, because they did not have the experience. There were thousands of unemployed Afrikaners. Hundreds of families were living in desperately poor conditions in the slums of the towns.

The government wanted to find jobs for these unemployed whites.

* The war was over, and the new government wanted to reconstruct white society. They were anxious to help Afrikaners to recover from the war.
* As the mines were very short of unskilled labour at this time, the government asked if unemployed whites could be used as unskilled workers on the mines.

UNSKILLED WHITE MINERS

In 1903, a mine manager named Cresswell tried to help jobless whites at the Village Main Reef Mine in Johannesburg. He gave them certain unskilled jobs for five shillings (50 cents) a day. This was more than twice as much as a black unskilled worker could earn. (The highest wage for a black worker was 22 1/2 cents a day.)

Cresswell hoped to show that whites could work better and harder than blacks. But Cresswell's experiments failed. The white workers could not produce more than twice as much ore as black workers.

Mine-owners found that if they paid unskilled whites five shillings a day, the mines would lose profits. It was cheaper and easier for mine-owners to employ blacks, so Cresswell's programme was stopped.

AFRIKANERS ENTER THE MINES

In 1907, the skilled miners went on strike. The mine-owners used hundreds of unemployed Afrikaners to break the strike. With the help of experienced black and Chinese miners, the labour of the Afrikaners kept the mines operating. They were given emergency lessons in rock drilling and given the role of 'supervising' black and Chinese drilling. From that time on, more and more Afrikaners joined the mines.

Within ten years, there were as many Afrikaners as there were English-speaking miners working on the Rand, and the special position of the early skilled miners was changed.

87

Chapter Sixteen

Black Workers' Resistance on the Mines

From the beginning, the struggle of black workers in South Africa was shaped by particularly difficult conditions. But the history of workers all over the world shows us that there are many ways in which exploitation can be resisted.

STRIKES

The clearest form of resistance is the strike. In a strike, workers unite to withdraw their labour — they refuse to work. The employer needs the workers to produce the goods that he sells — without their labour, his mine, factory or business cannot operate. If a strike is successful, the employer is forced to come to an agreement with the workers to improve their conditions.

A strike fails if the employer decides that he does not need to bargain with the workers. This can happen when:
* There are other workers ready to take the place of the strikers in the mine or factory. In times of great unemployment and poverty, for example, large numbers of people are desperate for jobs. They are usually prepared to work for the low pay that the strikers are fighting against. Workers who take the jobs of the strikers are called 'scabs'.

In the 1907 strike on the mines, unemployed Afrikaners 'scabbed' when skilled miners went on strike. White workers fought for job reservation because they were convinced that blacks would be happy to take over white jobs at lower pay — blacks could easily become 'scabs', argued the white workers, and 'scabs' could cause strikes to fail.
* Strikes also fail when the employer has the power to force the strikers back to work. Usually, this happens with the help of the government. The government sends the army and the police to stop the strike and

A scene from the 1920 black miners' strike — the biggest in the history of the Rand.

to 'restore order'.

Governments also support the employer by making laws to prevent strikes and to punish strikers. (For example in South Africa the State created the pass laws and the contract system to control workers and punish them if they stopped work without the employer's permission.)

So strikes do not usually succeed unless the workers have at least some power.
1. They need to have the power to prevent other workers from 'scabbing'. The skilled miners in the early mining years had this power — their skills were so scarce that no one else could replace them.
2. They need the power to organise in large numbers, as in trade unions. (If all workers went on strike, for example, there could be no scabbing.)
3. They need political power. In South Africa, the white workers used the vote to help get the Smuts government out after the

1922 strike.

INFORMAL RESISTANCE

When workers have very little power to improve their wages or working conditions, they often use other methods of protest. These methods are usually not direct. They are not obvious forms of protest. This other way of resisting is called *informal resistance.*

In South Africa in those early mining years (and in later years too) workers developed many kinds of informal resistance.

THE JOB BOYCOTT

* The simplest form of resistance was to look for better jobs in the first place. For example, after the Anglo-Boer War, thousands of black workers boycotted the mines because the mines dropped the wages. They

Resistance through strikes and desertion was punishable by law.

looked for work on the railways or in the towns instead. A government official in 1907 saw this very clearly. He said that the black worker 'would sooner go to the sea port and work for the harbour board or the diamond mines . . . failing that he comes to the Rand and, failing domestic service here, he goes on the mines. It is the most uncongenial class of work, and is practically the last resort of the native.'
* As one mine-owner said:

'The native method of striking is very simple. It must be remembered that he is not a permanent workman. He is always going home, and if he is not satisfied with conditions of employment, he simply does not come out again.'[1]

The boycott of the mines after the war led to a serious shortage of labour in the mines. The Chamber of Mines was forced to raise the wages of black workers slightly and they had to look outside South Africa for cheap labour.

DESERTION

* Another form of protest was *desertion*. Workers could not im-prove their jobs because it was against the law, so they simply left. We have seen in chapter 10 how the large number of deserters caused problems for the Chamber of Mines. Desertion continued in spite of the pass laws, the contract system, finger printing and other methods used to keep workers on the mines.

Desertion was highest in compounds where conditions were worst. For example, in 1908 a government report compared conditions at different mining compounds. Here is what the report said about the best and the worst compounds:
* *'Jumpers Mine: Standard of feeding, adequate. Soup issued in early morning. No punishment by stoppage of food. Very few cases of ill-treatment . . . Attitude of officials towards natives – good.'* The result was that only three men deserted the compound in 1908 out of 2 000 workers.
* *'Simmer Deep: Feeding only fairly adequate. No hot (drink) issued in the morning. Inefficients (loafers) punished by stoppage of meat rations. Several complaints received as to inaccurate marking of tickets . . . Continuous ill-treatment underground. Reasons for desertions, ill-treatment and unsympathetic attitude of officials.'*[2]

The result was that at Simmer Deep, 1 236 men deserted out of every 2 000 workers in 1908.

NON-COOPERATION

Many workers tried to limit their work by cooperating as little as possible. They deliberately worked badly, broke their tools and were careful not to do any more work than they had to.

The workers felt that they were being cheated. Firstly, their pay was so low. Secondly, they felt that they were tricked by the loafer ticket system and by broken promises. As one worker said:

'I drilled a hole, even if it was only 24 inches: I get no pay. But my master charges and blasts the hole all the same: and he gets paid for the rock broken by it.'[3]

A white mining engineer once tried to improve the work by offering to pay double for extra work. He said: *'I once tried it on the Ferreira Mine, and persuaded several boys to drill two holes instead of one. They were paid double for their work and we were all pleased, but they suddenly stopped, and when the*

A worker who was able to avoid the mines. His job was to look after the tramline points — his home, in Market Square, consisted of old boxes and tin from the rubbish dump.

mine foreman wanted to know why, they said: "It is all right putting in two holes now, but presently the boss will think that two holes is the day's work"... They saw what we were up to. They saw as well as some of the white men we have had to deal with, only the native was more honest about it. He stuck to it too.'[4]

Sometimes, workers managed to get less work done by pretending not to understand their orders. A lot of the time they really did not understand. White supervisors could not speak African languages and used 'fanagalo', which was nobody's language, anyway. But often workers very cleverly acted 'stupid'.

For these workers this was another form of resistance against doing work which they felt they were not paid for. They felt that the mine-owners, their managers and supervisors were cheating them. They did not have the power to organise themselves into unions. But there was little management could do about informal resistance.

BEATING THE SYSTEM

Some workers used the government's pass law system and the Chamber of Mines' recruiting system to find themselves better jobs. Men would join up with the WNLA recruiters and travel with the other mine-workers to the Rand mines. But they would secretly get off the train at Pretoria station. They would then apply for a pass at Pretoria and either get work there or travel to the Rand and look for jobs in the towns or in the better mines.

Workers got to know that the Pretoria pass offices were not as strict as the Rand. Pretoria was not marked as a labour area where Africans had to be jailed for six days to find out if they were deserters.

More and more people began to 'beat the system' in this way. One mining manager reported in 1902:

'It appears that particularly in the case of North Basothus and Tsongas they are well informed that on arriving in Pretoria, and making a statement that they wish to go to Johannesburg in order to find employment, passports are freely issued to them without question; they are fully conversant with the fact that this means they can obtain work in Johannesburg at higher rates of pay... officials assume that natives applying for passports have just arrived from their homes.'[5]

Those workers who were caught had to make statements. Here is the story of one deserter who tried to beat the pass system:

'I deserted from the New Unified on or about 20 November 1906 and proceeded to Pretoria on foot. When asked by the Pass Officer at Pretoria where I came from, I stated that I had been working for a contractor who had discharged me, and the following night I had been robbed, pass and everything taken from me. I was then given a travelling pass and I proceeded to Johannesburg by train.'[6]

ORGANISED RESISTANCE

After the Anglo-Boer War, more and more mine workers were caught for deserting or trying to get false passes. The new British government in the Transvaal made the pass laws stricter and trained more police to help control the mine's labour system.

But at the same time, mine workers were becoming more experienced. Migrant workers were beginning to understand the compound system and they could do their work in the mines better. As they became more experienced, mine workers also used more organised ways of protesting — namely through work-stoppages, or 'strikes'.

The earliest recorded black miners' strikes occurred in 1896, when the Mine Managers' Association decided to 'reduce wages, as it were, by force and at the point of the bayonet.'[7]

Just after the Anglo-Boer War there were a number of strikes. But in many of these, not all of the workers in any compound stopped working. Often a certain group of workers from the same tribe went on strike.

For example, one of the strikes on the mines was at Vereeniging Estate Coal Mine, in September 1901. One hundred and sixty-two Sotho workers refused to work unless they were paid for the five weeks that they had to wait at Aliwal North for rail permits. The recruiter had promised them that they would get paid for their time on the journey. But the manager said

they would only get their money at the end of the contract.

The workers decided to go home and crossed the Vaal River. Soldiers surrounded them and tried to force them to go back across the river. The workers armed themselves with sticks and stones so that they could escape. The soldiers shot nine workers dead and 15 were wounded.

There was another strike in the following year at the Geldenhuis Estate Mine where 448 Pedi workers went on strike.

They said that they had signed for a six-month contract and their contract was finished. They wanted to go home but the manager insisted that their contract still had another week to go, because they had not finished all their shifts. The strikers were arrested and sentenced to a two pound fine or one month's hard labour. The mining company offered to pay for the workers' fines if they came back to work on the mines to finish their contracts but more than a hundred workers refused, and went to jail instead.

Not all strikes were 'tribal' strikes. Sometimes all the workers in a compound acted together in solidarity. In the Langlaagte Deep Mine, the workers were very unhappy about the compound manager. In June 1902, 1 100 workers broke down the compound gates and marched to the Village Deep to complain about their treatment. Mounted police brought them back.

There were more strikes in the same year. All of them were stopped with the help of the army or the police.

Although wages were not improved, the strikes did cause some people from the British government to look at conditions in the compounds. The Chamber of Mines was forced to make some small improvements in the conditions of the compound workers.

During the next ten years we do not hear of black workers going on strike. Their bargaining power had been weakened by the importation of Chinese labour.

Strikers arrested during the 1913 strike.

1913 STRIKE

In 1913, black miners went on strike — in the same year as the white miners. When black miners tried to hold a meeting to discuss their complaints, policemen were called to stop the meeting. Leaders were arrested and sentenced to six months' hard labour. The strike grew.

Nine thousand compound workers in four mines refused to work. A notice was pinned on the office door of one compound to explain the workers' complaints. It said:

'We want to know what are the laws about our pay and our position in the compounds.'
'We do not see the miners who kick us underground. They are away and we have to work. Why should we be sent to work underground without knowing the black man's position?'[8]

The government called in the army and the compounds were surrounded. The workers were forced back to work — the strike failed.

Nevertheless, the Chamber of Mines was worried about the strike. Thirteen thousand black miners had struck in three days. They had acted together as workers and not just as tribesmen.

The mine-owners realised that black workers could disrupt production more effectively than white workers could. As one mine-owner said, the black worker was 'the true labourer of this country'.[9] Even if half the white miners went on strike, the black mine-workers could keep the mines going, as they had done during the white miners' strike in 1907.

The government set up a commission to look into the complaints of the mine-workers. The commission brought about a number of changes. Compound food, medical care and living conditions were improved. Working conditions in the mines also improved. For example, the mines had to put in larger lift cages and provide fires for heating while the workers were waiting to go down in winter time.

These changes improved the mine-worker's day-to-day life in many ways. But the problems of low wages and the system of labour control remained.

The basic complaints of black mine-workers continued.

GREATER HARDSHIPS

The reserves were getting more and more crowded after the Native Land Act of 1913. They were becoming poorer and less able to support their families. To make things worse, prices were rising. During the First World War, from 1914 to 1918, prices in South Africa nearly doubled. Yet black miners' wages stayed the same, while white miners' wages went up by 40%.

During the war, unrest amongst black workers continued. There were a number of strikes in the mines. Some mineworkers started to go to the Transvaal Native Congress and socialist meetings in the towns. It was then that the union of Industrial Workers of Africa was formed. It was led by men such as the journalist Saul 'Msane; Bud Mbelle, later to become a prominent member of the South African National Congress; Talbot Williams, also secretary of the largely 'coloured' African People's Organisation; and Grenon, editor of *Abantu Batho*, one of the first black newspapers in South Africa and the mouthpiece of the SANNC.

One police official reported:

'The natives have started holding meetings, resorting to picketing and are in fact organising in the same manner as the miners did on the 1913 and 1914 strikes.'[10]

But the police were always called. They arrested and jailed the leaders and the other workers were forced to go back to work.

BOYCOTT

By 1918 prices had gone up so much that the mine workers decided not to buy from compound stores — they boycotted the storekeepers because of high prices. For example:
* In 1913 an outfit of clothes cost R1,80 and boots cost R1,25.
* In 1918 the same clothes cost R3,80 and boots cost R2,00.

The SANNC deputation to London, 1918.
From left to right, back: J.C. Gumede, L.T. Mvabaza, R.V. Selope Thema.
Front: Solomon T. Plaatje, Rev. H. Ngcayinya.

The S.A.N.C.

— the forerunner of the ANC[26]

South Africa's first national movement was founded in January 1912. At a meeting in Bloemfontein there gathered royal chiefs from many parts of southern Africa, ministers, lawyers, teachers, clerks, leaders of the Transvaal and Natal Native Congress and other organisations from the Free State, the Cape and the Transvaal.

The meeting declared its aims: to unite all the different black organisations, as well as the many chiefdoms in South Africa.

'We are one people,' declared Pixley ka I. Seme, the founder of the movement, 'These divisions, these jealousies are the cause of all our troubles and of all our ignorance today.'[27]

Why was the SANNC formed in 1912? The new government of the Union of South Africa had passed a number of discriminatory laws against blacks.
- The 1911 *Native Labour Regulation Act* made it a crime for Africans to leave their jobs.
- The 1911 *Mines and Works Act* reserved skilled jobs for whites in the mines.
- The 1911 *Dutch Reform Church Act* excluded Africans from the DRC in the Transvaal and the OFS.
- The 1913 *Native Land Act,* limiting Africans' right to own land, was being prepared.

The SANNC aimed to speak to the government on behalf of the African people, demanding equal rights and justice for all. One of its first actions was to present a petition asking the government to stop the Land Act. The petition was politely received, but it failed to change the law.

Other petitions followed — to the British government, to the Peace Conference in Paris after the First World War, and several to the Prime Minister. These, too, failed.

Many people began to feel that the SANNC policy was not getting results. There were few workers in the organisation. It was led by educated men who believed in the power of words — one of their most outstanding achievements was the establishment of a national newspaper, *Abantu-Batho*. But the SANNC made little difference to the everyday lives of blacks in the early years.

The SANNC united the rulers of chiefdoms of South Africa. It also encouraged Africans to start seeing themselves as one nation. That was the most important achievement of the SANNC in the first years of its life.

The workers blamed the store-keepers for over-charging. But they were only partly right. Prices had gone up a lot during the war. At the same time, the stores continued to make high profits. The boycotts forced the mine managements to improve the compound stores, and some of the prices dropped a little. But the workers found that they still could not afford to buy what they needed.

They stopped the boycotts because they saw that what they needed was more pay to keep up with the higher cost of living. Their wages were worth even less than they had been before the war.

THE WAGE CAMPAIGN

In the same year as the boycott, white electricity and gas workers went on strike in Johannesburg. They forced the City Council to give them a 25 percent pay rise. Then black municipal workers followed their example. These were the 'bucket boys', who collected the refuse in buckets from the toilets of white families. They had the dirtiest and most unpleasant job in the country. They too were suffering from rising prices, and demanded a rise of sixpence a day.

However, the 'bucket boys' were not as successful as the white municipal workers. The black strikers were arrested under the Master and Servants Act for breaking their contracts, and sentenced to two months' labour. They had to do the same jobs as before, and as their punishment they had to work without pay for two months. They were watched by an armed guard, ready to shoot if they tried to run away or did not do their work properly.

Blacks on the Rand were furious at this treatment of the workers. The Transvaal Congress, the African People's Organisation and the Industrial Workers of Africa held angry meetings to call for action.
* 'God gave you Africa to live in,' said one Congress speaker to a meeting of about 1 000 people. 'He gave you anything he knew was necessary for you. He gave you a land and gold which you gave to other people ... Today you are carrying passes. Today you have got no place. Today they are telling you that you will get a place in heaven. There is one thing sure my friends, it is this, if you have no place on earth you will have no place in heaven.'11

The next day, after a meeting of about 10 000 people, the flag was torn up. Cars and trams were stopped. A riot nearly started.
* Congress and the APO called for a general strike for 'a shilling a day' increase in all black workers' wages and a general strike for higher wages.

The IWA

The First African Trade Union

The Industrial Workers of Africa (the IWA) was the first African trade union in South Africa. It was formed early in 1918 and was to play an important part in the restless post-war period of black resistance. Influenced by the largely white International Socialist League, the IWA claimed to be 'not a political body but an industrial organisation', whose aims were to organise the workers and plan strike action for higher pay.

The IWA printed pamphlets in Sotho and Zulu for the workers: *'There is only one way to freedom, black workers. Unite as workers, unite!'* it urged. *'Forget the things that divide you. Let there be no longer any talk of Basuto, Zulu or Shangaan. You are all labourers, Let labour be your common bond.'28*

IWA members travelled along the Reef, organising workers in the compounds. They influenced the Transvaal Congress, pushing it towards more militant action and towards workers' concerns for a while. In later years an open split developed between the two organisations. While Congress leaders accused the IWA of being dominated by white communists, the IWA criticised the TNC for its middle-class leaders, who refused to see what lay behind the racist system in South Africa, neglecting the interest of the workers.

The IWA was eventually overtaken in the 1920s by the ICU (see page 98) and the Non-European Trade Union Federation.

Mass meeting at Newtown, calling for a strike.

'The white workers do not write to the Governor-General when they want more pay. They strike and get what they should. Why should we not do the same?' said a Congress leader.[12]

The response to the call was great — but the workers were unorganised. The Prime Minister, Louis Botha decided to hold a meeting with members of the Congress. He promised that he would see what could be done about the low wages. He set up a commission to look into the wages of black workers. In return, the Transvaal Congress agreed to call off the strike.

But the Prime Minister's Commission did not support higher wages for all black workers. They said that the wages of the compound workers in the mines did not need to go up. Workers got free board and lodging and the higher cost of living 'was not causing serious hardship' to compound workers.[13]

In the meantime, some mine-workers went on with their strike. As they had been locked up in their compounds, they did not know that the strike. had been called off.

On 1 July black miners from Crown Mines, Robinson Deep and Ferreira Deep refused to work unless they got higher pay. Mine managers called in the police and the strikers were forced down the shafts at gun point. Leaders of the ISL, including Cetyiwe, Letanka and Mvabasa were arrested.

So the wage campaign failed. But workers continued to fight for higher wages in other ways.

ANTI-PASS CAMPAIGN

People began to turn their attention to the labour system in general. They began to say that low wages were part of the whole system of labour control, and to call for a 'free labour system'.

'The object of the contract system is to obtain cheap and forced labour,' said the Transvaal Congress in a statement ot the government.[14]

'The Pass Law is nothing but

SCENES FROM THE ANTI-PASS CAMPAIGN, 1919.

(Above) Outside the pass office, men collect discarded passes in large sacks.
(Below) Resisters march to the pass office to hand in their passes.

slavery and forced labour. It was made to force the natives to work,' said the Vice-President of the Congress, D.S. Letanka, to the Minister of Justice.[15]

'There is one thing that binds us down, and that is the Pass Law, and that law we must abolish. We must organise all the natives, after which we can fight not by arms and killing anyone but by striking for what we want,' declared H. Phooko, Chairman of the Industrial Workers of Africa.[16]

At a big meeting one day in 1919 workers decided to take action against the pass laws. About 1 000 men marched to the Johannesburg pass office and handed in their passes.

The police began to arrest leaders. But people continued to organise. 'We must all be leaders,'[17] as one speaker said. Groups of Africans organised themselves and spread the anti-pass campaign to other parts of the Rand. Bags of passes were collected all over the Rand and handed in at pass offices.

As the meetings continued, fights broke out between workers and police. Hundreds more Africans were arrested.

Meanwhile, the unrest on the mines continued. On 6 November 1919, 300 mineworkers marched to Johannesburg from Rose Deep Mines in Germiston to protest about their food. The next month, workers boycotted the New Modder-fontein compound stores. Worried, the Chamber of Mines called in chiefs from the reserves to come and talk to the men in the compounds and ask them

not to 'cause trouble' because their families needed their wages.

A month later the Chamber also instructed mine managers to raise the top wages of black workers from two shillings (20 cents) to two shillings and three pence (22½ cents) a shift. The Chamber also announced that all workers who worked 180 shifts continuously without staying away for sickness would get a bonus of five shillings (50 cents).

However, some mines gave the rise to the workers and some did not. Those who did not get the increase became even angrier. In any case, black miners felt that these improvements in pay were too little and came too late.

MINERS' STRIKE

Work stoppages continued in mines along the Rand.

There was evidence of organised resistance by the IWA. At the Consolidated Main Reef mine, in compound No. 3, for example, a Native Constable Arthur reported that he saw *'a strange well dressed native there in No. 40 Room lecturing to about 25 others upon the benefits they would enjoy if they would all unite against their employers and refuse to work until they got their rights.'*[18]

The District Commandant of the East Rand reported that 'at present there are 24 educated natives visiting the Reef compounds who deliver leaflets and preach socialist propaganda to the mine natives.'[19]

Then on 16 February 1920 two Zulu miners, Mobu and Vilikati, were arrested on an East Rand Property mine for moving around in the Cason compound, urging workers to stay away from work. The next day, 25 000 Cason compound workers went on strike.

They refused to go back to work unless
* the two arrested men were released;
* there was an increase of three shillings a day in wages to keep up with the rising cost of living;
* there were certain improvements in the working conditions.

The strike quickly spread to other parts of the Rand, to other mines on the East Rand, through to Johannesburg and along the West Rand as well. In the 12 days the strike lasted, about 71 000 black miners went on strike and 21 mines had to stop working during this time.

It was the largest strike in the history of South Africa. The President of the Chamber of Mines said that the strike had 'practically paralysed the industry.'

'There was for the first time,' he continued, 'a native strike in the true sense of the word . . . an absolutely peaceful cessation of work.'[20]

But the Chamber of Mines and the government did not respond peacefully to the strike. The mine-owners refused to raise the wages of black miners. They said it was impossible to give even the smallest wage increases. They argued that mines would lose their profits if expenses went up. One mine owner said that if wages increased to three shillings, 23 mines would have to close down. The mining industry would be finished.

The army was rushed in to surround the compounds. The strikers were told to make their complaints. Those who spoke were handcuffed and arrested as the 'ringleaders'.

The townships produced politically conscious men and women.

One striker at Knights Deep Mine said: *'The White man goes below, does no work and gets big money. The African gets all the gold out of the ground and gets very little money. How is that fair? The extra three pence (2½ cents) a day is not enough.'*[21] He was arrested.

Workers were ordered to get back to work or they would be sent to jail. All over the Rand, workers were beaten and driven down the shafts.

The compounds were dealt with one at a time. Workers were told that the men in the other compounds had gone back to work. One by one, the compounds were subdued by the managers and the army.

Then only Village Deep compound was left. Workers refused to go underground. The army tried to force them but the workers still refused to work. The strikers cut down trees and armed themselves with sticks. When soldiers broke into the compound and fired on the strikers, three were killed and 40 were wounded. The remaining workers went back to work. The strike was over.

RESULTS

It was 25 years before so many mineworkers went on strike again. The mine-owners had used all their power to crush the resistance of the workers. But once again, the strike had the Chamber of Mines and the government worried. They saw that the workers had been organised and united. They were also aware of the growing numbers of black workers living with their families in the towns. Many of these townspeople were joining political organisations. The Transvaal Congress, for example, had played a part in the strike, sending letters of protest to the government and holding meetings with workers in Witwatersrand towns.

Said one police inspector, *'The cause of this strike is purely industrial, due to increased costs of living . . . (But) if some steps are not taken, it will be playing*

Scenes from

(Top right) Mounted police outside the compound. (Middle right) Police confront workers at the compound gate. (Bottom right) The compound gate is closed to keep the workers inside.
(Below) Police and soldiers 'persuade' compound workers to abandon the strike.

the 1920 Strike

into the hands of the native agitators and so-called National Congress which will undoubtedly bring about another strike, probably much better organised than this which may have the most serious results.'[22]

* Both the government and the Chamber of Mines were concerned about black workers' growing awareness that they had power in numbers. 'You cannot imprison millions,' the resisters declared during the anti-pass campaign.[23] Black workers as well as the more educated teachers, ministers and traders were beginning to protest together.

The Chamber of Mines and the government were determined to prevent strikes in future and to assert their control over black townsmen. They did this in a number of ways:

* The government tightened up the pass laws for blacks living in towns. And even if people did have their passes in order, they could be sent away to the reserves if they were found to be 'idle, disorderly or dissolute' — in other words, if they were 'troublemakers'. The government also passed a law that all contracts for black workers in towns must be registered.

* The Chamber of Mines was not prepared to raise the wages of black workers. But it did realise that black miners had real grievances which could not be suppressed by force. So it tried to improve workers' conditions in small ways.

A few months after the strike the Chamber of Mines asked all compounds to improve their food, for example. Some did, but some did not, saying they could not afford to spend any more money on food.

The Chamber of Mines also started a black newspaper for those clerks and workers who could read. The newspaper said it aimed 'to educate white and black and to point out their respective duties... to foster a spirit of give and take, to promote the will to co-operate, to emphasise the obligations of black and white to themselves and to each other.'[24]

(Top left) Workers gather inside the compound. (Middle left) The amy surrounds a compound. (Bottom left) Police supervise the confiscation of strikers' sticks and kieries.
(Below) Arrested strikers are marched from the compound by mounted police.

The Chamber of Mines hoped to draw the most able blacks away from thoughts of organising workers and demanding higher pay. The Chamber decided to give more of the semi-skilled jobs to blacks, because they wanted black workers to feel that there were real opportunities for them on the mines.

'The semi-skilled native justly treated should prove a useful asset to the industry in assisting to guide the mass of unskilled labourers,' argued mine offici-als.[25] In other words, the mine-owners hoped to be able to separate the most able workers from the others, thus 'buying them off'. If they were promoted, they might stop 'causing trouble' amongst the rest of the workers.

The strike therefore made the mine-owners decide to loosen the job colour bar slightly. It was partly this move that led to the white miners' strike of 1922. And it was the 1922 strike that brought down the Smuts government.

The fall of Smuts in 1924 marked the end of an era — after this date, more and more capitalists made their wealth from other industries — from factories, from property, from business and from commercial farming. Although the mine-owners continued to be very powerful from 1924, they had to share this power more and more with other, growing interest groups.

THE ICU – THE BLACK RESPONSE TO THE TURBULENT TWENTIES

The ICU started off as a dockworkers' union in Cape Town in 1919. After a 400–strong strike later that year, the movement developed into a general union for black workers under the name *Industrial and Commercial Workers Union of Africa* with the founder, Clements Kadalie, as its secretary.

The early 1920's were years of up-heaval and hardship for blacks in South Africa. The rising prices since the war and the overcrowded land resulted in more people being forced to become migrant workers. Unrest amongst the low-paid farm workers, strikes, riots and evictions from people's homes were common.

Against this background, the ICU grew rapidly. By 1927, it boasted 100 000 members, workers in the towns and on the farms.

One of the most important achievements of the ICU was to stop black labourers being dipped like cattle when they entered the municipality of Durban. But the movement did not make any other positive gains for its members. Although its numbers were high, ICU organisation was weak and lacked a clear direction. Faced by government persecution, the leadership split between the activists and the 'hamba kahle' group. There were also regional diffences. A.W.G. Champion formed his own break–away ICU in Natal.

The ICU began to decline after 1927. By the end of the decade the great mass movement was no more.

(Top right) The letterhead of the Industrial and Commercial Worker's Union.
(Middle right) The leaders of the ICU.
(Bottom right) General Smuts inspects black troops during World War I — black soldiers were not permitted to carry guns. The Smuts government was ousted from power in 1924 by the Afrikaner National Party.

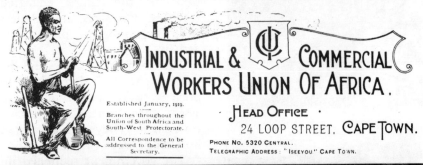

THERE IS FIRE HERE "I.C.U. Chiefs"

Chapter Seventeen

The Divided Workers

'We dig the gold out of the mines, but when it comes to be divided, we are not wanted. There are two nations here — black and white.'

— Congress leader, Mvabaza, January 1919.[1]

We have seen how the workers were divided into two groups:
* a small group of white workers whose wages were high;
* a very large group of black workers whose wages were very low.
Both groups were workers. Both groups were forced to leave their land and become wage—earners in the mines. But they were divided.

This chapter is a brief summary of the reasons why workers in South Africa came to be separated by the mine-owners. (The mine-owners did this to safeguard their profits and to protect their system of labour control.)

WHY MINE-OWNERS PREFERRED BLACK LABOUR

Mine-owners preferred to employ blacks. They preferred black workers for several reasons:
* Mine-owners argued that black workers could survive on two shillings a day because they had compounds to house and feed them and the reserves helped to support their families.
* Unlike black workers, whites were able to settle in the towns. There they had to find housing and food — which were not provided by the mine-owners. They relied completely on their wages to support their families, but as we have seen, they were able to demand and get higher wages.

'The native is able in unskilled work to sell his labour at a price at which a white cannot live,' said a government commission in 1903.[2]
* Blacks were in a weak position. They had to accept whatever wages they could get.
* Poor, unskilled whites had more power than black workers. We have seen in Chapter 15 that white workers' voting power helped to topple the Smuts government in 1924. White workers also had trade union rights which were denied to black workers. Furthermore, white workers were free of the workers—pass laws and other systems of labour control that the mine-owners imposed on black workers. Whites were therefore free of the wage colour bar. They could demand — and get — higher wages.

Mine-owners tried as far as possible to employ black workers. They justified this policy by claiming that whites were bad workers because they did not know how to take orders and were too soft to do the hard labour of the unskilled miner. They refused to give unskilled jobs to whites, saying that unskilled work was 'native's work'.

'I myself prefer getting a native to do native's work,' said one employer in 1913, 'because I have less trouble with him.'[3]

Another employer said that black unskilled workers were easier to control than whites. 'You can deal with the Kaffir very much as you like,' he said, quite openly.[4]

99

WORKERS SEPARATED

The mine-owners were also careful not to give the black and white workers a chance to act together against management. Managers saw how the 1913 strike by whites encouraged black workers to try the same methods of striking and picketing.

'If a large number of White men are employed on the Rand in the position of labourers,' wrote one mine-owner, 'the same trouble will arise as in the Australian colonies.' (He meant that the Australian workers had organised trade unions.) 'The combination of the working classes will become so strong as to be able more or less to dictate, not only on the question of wages, but also on political questions by the power of the vote.'[5]

Mine-owners felt it was important to distance white miners from the black workers, and to place one above the other.

'The white miner is more a shift-boss than a miner proper, being required to take charge of gangs of natives, superintend work and get as much out of them as possible,' wrote the editor of the *SA Mining Journal* in 1893.

'We do not want a White (working class) in this country,' said the powerful mine-owner. Cecil John Rhodes, 'The position of the Whites among the vastly more numerous Black population requires that even their lowest ranks should be able to maintain a standard of living far above the poorest sections of the population of a purely White country.'[6]

The white workers were only a small group of miners. The mine-owners could afford to give them higher wages than they paid for labouring jobs.

The black miners kept the mines going. It was more important to keep them under control and their wages low. So white workers were gradually given more and more supervisory work. They did less and less of the actual mining themselves.

Although they were workers themselves, white supervisors had direct power over black workers. They issued loafer tickets, policed the workers underground and generally came to represent for blacks the mine-owners' control over labour.

The system of labour control also produced collaborators.

'In this country, the white miner is more a shift boss than a miner proper, being required to take charge of gangs of natives, superintend their work and get as much out of them as possible.'

— *SA Mining Journal, 1893*

By 1924, most white miners underground were mainly doing the work of supervising black workers.

DIVISION BY RACE

The separation of workers according to race was welcomed by white workers. They regarded themselves as 'higher' than the black workers, even if they were 'lower' than the other white groups in South Africa. Why was this?

Most white South Africans were brought up to believe that they were better than blacks — in other words, they were *racists,* because they thought that one race was better than another.

Racism in South Africa goes back a long way. By the time gold was discovered, most of South Africa's land had already been conquered by whites. To justify taking the land, many whites said that they deserved the land. They claimed superiority over blacks, whom they had defeated. They were stronger than blacks with the help of horses and guns.

Centuries of *slavery* and *colonialism* lay behind this feeling of superiority.

(See box and pictures on this page).

When whites became workers, this racism continued. Racism divided the workers. We have seen how white workers came to fear the cheap labour of the blacks. They spoke of the danger of being 'pulled down to Kaffir wages' and fought for the job colour bar to protect their positions and separate them from the black workers. Racism helped semi-skilled whites to get higher wages. These whites called themselves 'civilised' because they were white — and argued that they deserved 'civilised' high wages.

(Top right) A plan of a slave-trading ship bound for the plantations of North and South America and the West Indies. The slaves were carefully 'packed' so that hardly a square centimetre was wasted.

The History of Racism

Racism did not start in South Africa. Many Europeans had racist ideas before the first whites arrived at the Cape in 1652. European countries like England, Portugal and Spain became rich through the slave trade. Millions of slaves from Africa were taken to north and south America to work in the sugar and cotton plantations there. Of course, slaves were not paid for their work — they were bought by their masters and put to work in the same way as oxen are today. They were treated as property — like animals, not like people.

The slaves were black. The masters were white. Whites thought of themselves as born to be masters because of their skin colour.

In the 18th and 19th centuries, European countries began to establish factories. These factories needed raw materials to process and sell. They began to look for other countries which could supply these raw materials. For example, they needed warm climates to grow cotton, rubber, tea, coffee and sugar.

Britain conquered India, north America and parts of Africa after much fighting and resistance from these countries. Most of the rest of Africa was taken by France (who also conquered Indo-China). Portugal and Spain also took parts of Africa (in addition to their colonies in South America).

The control of one country over another is known as *colonialism*. By the end of the 19th century, a large part of the world was colonised by Europeans.

The British, for example, boasted of an empire so big that the sun was always shining on some part of it.

The colonisers began to think of themselves as the 'superior race', and looked down on darker skinned people as the 'lesser breeds'. They began to believe that they were 'helping' their colonies by bringing 'civilisation' to them — teaching them Christianity, teaching them to read and write and to wear European clothes. But while the colonised people benefited in some ways, these changes meant that they began to *need* clothes, books, transport and often food and drink made in Europe. Europe's factories grew richer from their colonies. while the colonies themselves grew poorer.

In South Africa, the most blatant racism is expressed by those whites who feel threatened by blacks in the competition for land, jobs and wealth. But racism goes deeper than aggressive behaviour and insulting words. The history of colonisation shows us that racists often congratulate themselves for 'advancing' the 'developing' peoples, while extracting profits at their expense.

A scene in 19th-century Africa. Slavery, conquest and colonialism set the black man against his brother, weakening the continent still further.

THE MINE-OWNERS AND RACISM

Racism helped the mine-owners too. South Africa was a colonial society, where blacks had been weakened by the loss of their land. The mine-owners profited from this weakness, forcing blacks into cheap labour.

Racism gave them another excuse for paying blacks low wages and keeping them under control. Racism helped mine-owners and managers to believe that blacks were not the same as other people. One mine-owner, for example, gave a speech to his company in 1903. He spoke of the black worker as a 'muscular machine' — who did the hard labour on the mines, while the white worker — he claimed — did the brain work.[7] It suited mine-owners very well at that stage to see blacks as machines, without feelings or brains — this made it easier to excuse the low wages they got.

Many mine-owners and managers liked to think of blacks as backward and lazy, or otherwise as children.

'The position of Kaffirs is in many respects like children,' wrote the editor of the mine-owners' journal, the *South African Mining Journal* in 1892.[8] Both children and blacks needed 'special control and supervision when exposed to temptations'.[9] The black worker could not be allowed to 'roam unrestricted, not improbably (drunk), at his own sweet will.'[10] Blacks needed to be put into compounds for their own sakes, concluded the editor.

A mine-owner warned: 'We should not over-pamper the native and thus weaken his naturally strong constitution.'[11]

In these ways mine-owners used racism to justify the treatment of their workers.

Racism, therefore, resulted in direct benefits for both classes of whites — in the form of higher profit for the capitalists and higher-paid, protected jobs for the white workers.

Racism was used to justify the bad conditions in the compounds. Said the chairman of the Rand Mines: 'In their own kraals natives in general live in a more or less backward state of civilisation, and there is in my opinion a danger that we may be going too far in our endeavours to make them comfortable, and I think that the natives far prefer those compounds which are not too well-ventilated and airy.'[12]

South African mineworkers, shoulder to shoulder — yet deeply divided.

'We are fighting our own battles and the white man is fighting his own battle. He does not consider us and we do not consider him in this respect, if I may say so.'
— (A.W.G. Champion, 1925)[13]

There was a widespread feeling on the part of the blacks that white workers were using their power in a selfish way. The job colour bar was merely a form of protection against the mine-owners' control over black workers. White workers did nothing to help liberate blacks from the forced labour system, which was the real cause of their own insecurity. Few black workers therefore felt any sympathy for the whites' struggle for trade union rights.

A group of professional and business men. In South Africa, the middle class was reserved for whites only. Blacks were excluded from opportunities to advance themselves. Soon after the discovery of minerals they were barred from owning mining fields or licences; from the right to trade in diamonds and gold; from owning a shop or being 'in any way connected with the working of the gold mines, except as a working man in the service of whites.'[14]

The whites-only parliament.

To sum up, then: in South Africa, racism developed with the conquest of the land. This racism continued into industrial times, and was used by the mine-owners to justify the treatment of black workers.

A pattern of race discrimination emerged.

* Whites settled in the towns — but black miners were migrant workers.
* Whites were free from the pass laws and other forms of labour control. Black workers were not.
* White workers had strong bargaining power — black workers did not.

* Blacks, therefore, were paid ultra-low wages — whites were not.

So it came about that the workers of South Africa were divided by race, and South Africa's special form of racial capitalism was established.

103

Conclusion

The Price of Progress

This book ends in 1924, when the Pact Government came into power. An age was coming to an end — an age in which the needs of the mine-owners dominated South Africa. The two parties of the new government — the Afrikaner National Party and the South African Labour Party — opposed the power of the mine-owners. From this time on, other white interest groups would also have their say in the running of the country. Commercial farmers, factory owners and even white workers had representatives in the government. And although the mine-owners remained powerful, they now had to share their power with South Africa's other capitalist groups.

The first quarter of this century was an important and formative period — it laid down the foundations of the system we live in today. For it was during this time that South Africa's industrial revolution developed. In this last chapter we examine the legacy left to South Africa by the Rand mines and their owners.

PROGRESS

'The most gigantic mining industry the world has seen.'
— S.A. Mining Journal,
1 October 1898.

The short period of history that we have been studying was one of dramatic change. In forty years, for example, the population of Johannesburg reached half a million. In 1930, with the price of gold still fixed at £4,28 an ounce, the mining companies made R90 million in profit.

The economy of South Africa rested on gold. Directly or indirectly half the population depended on gold.

The gold mines on the Rand advanced the study of science and expanded man's knowledge of the earth. Geologists, who study the formation of rock, learned to follow the hidden seams of gold underground. They advised the mine-owners where to sink the shafts. Machines and chemicals were developed to drill the ore, blast it, crush it, wash it, separate the gold from it; to purify the gold, melt it and pour it into trays to harden. Scientists in the service of the mine-owners were constantly working on new ways of saving costs — the invention of the jack-hammer, for example, revolutionised rock-breaking underground, and dramatically increased the production of gold.

Gold stimulated other industries, too. The coal mines were developed, providing a plentiful

source of power for the mines' machines, and for transport. Roads, railways and shipping improved to serve the Rand. Travel became quicker and safer; goods could be transported more cheaply to the towns.

More efficient methods of farming and improved transport resulted in large, commercial farms producing more food to sell to the townspeople and the mining compounds. The mines also attracted capital to South Africa for other projects, such as the development of a supply of cheap electricity for the Rand.

What was started for the sake of the mines, then, developed the capitalist economy generally, encouraging the growth of towns and factories. The wealth of the Rand mines resulted in a modern capitalist state, politically and economically united under one government.

THE PRICE OF PROGRESS

These features are generally described as 'progress'. But progress came at a high price — it brought human misery and displacement to hundreds of thousands of people. For in order to make the gold mines profitable, the mine-owners had to change the methods of production and labour in South Africa, revolutionising the social system itself.

* Firstly, they had to destroy the old, land-based economy of pre-industrial times and replace it with a basic capitalist system — one of employers and wage-earning workers.
* To meet their massive labour needs, the mine-owners had to create a labour force by destroying the independence of the black farmer and removing most of his land, so that he would be driven to work for wages.
* To maximise their profits and minimise their labour costs, the mine-owners had to suppress the rights of the workers to organise and bargain. The chart on this page summarises the ways in which the mine-owners developed the wage colour bar — the system of labour control that kept the wages low for the vast majority, the black workers.
* In order to make these revolutionary changes, the mine-owners needed enormous power. They organised themselves into a united front, through the Chamber of Mines, and obtained the support of the government and people with influence. We have seen how they achieved these aims in Section II of this book. The mine-owners thus became important members of the ruling class.

The Wage Colour Bar

How Labour Control Of Black Workers Led To Low Wages

SYSTEM OF CONTROL FOR WORKERS

1. Migrant Labour — Migrant workers worked far from their homes, in the mines and the towns. They left their families behind and after six or 12 months, they came home again for a time.

2. The Compounds — Mine workers were housed and fed in compounds. They needed a pass each time they left the compound.

3. The Contract System — A black worker could not start working in the mines without a contract. It was a crime to try to change a worker's contract in any way. A worker could not try to raise his wages, or stay away from work.

4. The Pass Laws — (a) African men were not allowed on the Rand without passes. To look for work they had to get passes. They were allowed to look for work in certain labour districts only. (b) They were given three to six days to find work. Otherwise they had to leave.

5. The Maximum Wage System — Black unskilled workers on the mines could not get more than twenty-two and a half cents for a ten hour shift. This wage stayed more or less the same for 30 years.

6. The Recruiting System — The Chamber of Mines recruited cheap labour from poorer countries. This helped to stop the shortage of cheap labour. When there was less labour shortage, it was even easier to keep wages down.

HOW IT WORKED FOR THE MINE-OWNERS

Migrant labour kept wages down — mine-owners maintained that migrant workers did not need high wages because their families were already living on the land.

The employers maintained that as compound workers got free board and lodging their wages were lower. It was also easier to control workers in compounds.

Under the contract system the employer had a great deal of power over his employee. Once a worker started to work, he lost his power to bargain for higher wages or better conditions at work.

(a) The pass laws forced people to look for jobs in districts where employers wanted labour. (b) The quickest way to find a job was on the mines, where the pay was usually lowest. The pass system therefore assisted the mines in obtaining cheap labour.

The Chamber of Mines agreed not to compete for labour — all the mining companies paid black workers a maximum wage. If any mine paid more than the maximum wage, the mine-owners had to pay a fine to the Chamber of Mines. In this way, black miners' wages were kept low.

Black workers in South Africa were not free to move around the towns and offer their labour for the best wages; or settle with their families in the towns; or bargain for higher wages and better working conditions. They were forced to work under a powerful system of labour control, at ultra-low wages, thus increasing the mine-owner's profits.

'A course of six to twelve months on the mines is the best education for the natives. Here they can learn the value of discipline, regularity and the ways of the white man.'[1]

'Outside of the special reserves, the ownership of the land must be in the hands of the white race. The surplus of young men must earn their living by working for a wage.'[2]

'Thorough and general eviction of natives from private property through the country would effectually dispose of labour troubles as it would force upon the market the excess population and thus create a floating population of native labourers dependent upon it for its support.'[3]

'That the native is grossly overpaid is undeniable.'[4]

CHAMBER OF MINES
PRESIDENT'S ADDRESS
MARCH 1912

Were they evil men?

These are the words of powerful men. Admired, praised and envied by members of their own class, the mine-owners were an important part of a system of forced labour, starvation wages, increasing poverty and loss of land, and a deeply divided working class. Were they evil men?

The aim of this book is to understand the forces of history, not merely to condemn the individual actors who walk across the stage. Like most people, the mine-owners tended to see what they wanted to see, and to believe what suited them. They liked to think that the gold mines were bringing 'progress' to the country as a whole and 'civilisation' to the workers. It was convenient to claim that the shocking living and working conditions in the mines were better for the workers than the subsistence life they lived on the land.

As friends, husbands and fathers, some of these mine-owners may have been kindly and decent men — perhaps they even genuinely believed that for migrant workers the compound was 'like a club'.

But whether they believed what they said or not, they behaved as they did because they were mine-owners. Like the rest of us, they were the products of a *system* in which they occupied a particular class position.

As capitalists, they needed to make maximum profits at the least possible expense.

As we saw in Chapter 5, two factors in particular led them to exploit the worker even more. The deep-level mining of low grade ore was costly; the fixed price of gold meant that these additional costs could not be passed on to the buyer. The only way in which they could maintain high profits was by 'ultra-exploitation' of the workers — by reducing their wages still further and extracting as much work out of them as possible.

The Industrial Revolution in England

In different parts of the world at different times, the growth of capitalism and industrialisation have produced effects similar to those which South Africa also experienced — men have been forced to leave their land and sell their labour for wages.

England was one of the first countries to go through the upheaval of the industrial revolution. Powerful landlords caused laws to be made to force small farmers off the land. These men, deprived of their means of production — their land — were forced to move to the towns, the factories and the mines to sell the only thing they had left to sell — their labour.

Over a period of about 200 years, England changed from a land economy to an industrial, capitalist system. In that time, power was transferred from the wealthy landlords to the new capitalist class — coal-mine owners, factory owners, traders and ship owners, profiting from the labour of workers, both in Britain and the colonies.

The new social system created a class of capitalists and a large class of workers. As in South Africa, the 'upper' classes tended to think of themselves as superior to the workers. They spoke about the 'dirty', 'lazy' and 'ignorant' working class. They reasoned that the workers must be inferior, otherwise they would not be poor. They regarded the *results* of poverty — crime, violence, drink and ignorance — as the *causes* of poverty.

British employers saw themselves as the 'teachers', for they had the 'brains', while they called workers 'hands' — it was the worker's duty in life to provide labour, they felt. That was how God made the world and people must not upset this order.

'Nothing is more favourable to morals than learning to take orders early in life, hard work and regular working hours,' declared a Mr G.A. Lee, a cotton factory owner in the 19th century, who employed children from 6 o'clock in the morning to 8 o'clock at night.[5] It was hardly surprising that this capitalist's idea of 'morality' and goodness also happened to result in the most productive and obedient work force — and bigger profits.

Children were used as labourers in the English coal mines.

(Above) British police break up a demonstration of workers, 1847. The nineteenth century was a period of rapid industrial growth and labour resistance.

The Colonial Heritage

In South Africa the mine-owners developed a capitalist system — one that was closely related to the country's colonial history. When minerals were discovered, there was a ready-made situation which the mine-owners were able to exploit.

South Africa was a conquered land. Black farmers had been dispossessed of most of their land and were in a vulnerable position. The mine-owners were able to take advantage of the dispossessed in order to create a massive and cheap labour force.

South Africa's colonial history gave rise to a violent and racist society which suited the mine-owners very well. Nineteenth century employers in England justified exploitation of their workers by regarding them as an inferior class. South African employers justified exploitation of *their* workers by regarding them as an inferior race.

Race was seen as the dividing line. Yet the mine-owners were not only white: they were also capitalists. And the 'cheap labour' was not only black but was also a growing, potentially powerful working class.

One of Bambata's men killed in the field, 1906. The 'Bambata Rebellion' was one of the last acts of resistance by a chief to colonialism. Thousands of men and women under Bambata in Natal refused to pay increased taxes. The uprising was ruthlessly crushed by the British colony of Natal. After that, resistance increasingly took the form of labour and political movements in the urban areas.

A compound dormitory in Crown Mines, during demolition, showing the concrete shelves or 'bunks' upon which workers had to sleep. Workers were housed in this compound until 1979. (Photo: Les Lawson)

The Birth of a Working Class

What was the situation of the first generation of black workers on the Rand?

In this early period, there was little organisation. We have seen how, already weakened by the loss of land and the gradual destruction of the traditional economy of the chiefdoms, men came from all over southern Africa to work under strange conditions. Few were full-time workers — as we know, the migrant labour system kept most black workers tied to the land. Men who spent most of their working lives on the mines still regarded themselves mainly as farmers, belonging to a chiefdom rather than a working class.

Nevertheless, during this period workers were already beginning to realise that their struggle was changing from a struggle over land to a fight for higher wages. Ironically, the migrant system, which prevented black workers from uniting, was also the source of their strength. Migrants were able to use their land base to boycott the Rand mines after the Anglo-Boer War, by staying at home. Formal resistance, too, was taking place as early as 1896.

The mine-owners responded to this early resistance by tightening up their labour system. In chapters 11 and 13 we saw how they introduced the compounds as a form of control soon after the early strikes and the coming of the Chinese indentured labourers. We saw, too, how pass laws and other forms of labour control were made more effective after the war, in response to workers' resistance. Then the 1913 Land Act removed from most blacks the possibility of relying entirely on the land to survive.

Worker and black national consciousness developed as South Africa's economy expanded, especially during and after the First World War. A black population employed outside the mines was growing in the towns. The South African Native National Congress had been established in 1912, and its Transvaal branch took up workers' issues.

South African mineworkers were not only divided along racial lines. Migrant labour and the compound system kept black workers divided among themselves. In the compounds migrant workers preferred to be with friends from home, and mine managers encouraged this separation along ethnic lines. Compound police, for example, were chosen from the ranks of Zulu workers. The result of this policy was division and hostility between workers of different chiefdoms.

Its members, as well as other groups, campaigned for higher wages and against the pass laws. Black workers became more experienced and organised: their resistance culminated in the massive mine-workers' strike in 1920, which shook the labour system even though it failed to change it.

As for the white workers, their struggle against the powerful mine-owners centred mainly around their own job insecurity.

This was caused by the racial exploitation of black workers — the wage colour bar — and resulted in an unequal and racial division of the workers.

Yet the relationship between white and black workers was not always negative — the white workers' strike of 1913, for example, politicised black miners, inspiring them to examine their own forms of resistance. There is evidence, too, of communication between black wor-

kers and the socialists of the day — those 'agitators', black and white, who preached resistance against the capitalists and unity amongst all workers.

For the most part, however, the class struggle took on a racial form, and the mine-owners were able quite easily to buy off the white workers with protected jobs and higher wages, dividing them from the rest of the working class.

In this book, we have seen that the history of South Africa in the first quarter of this century was not the history of the mine-owners alone. Their supremacy was challenged by the workers in many ways. It is true that this resistance failed to change the basic system of labour control, or to raise the ultra-low wages of the black workers. But out of resistance grew a worker consciousness. The mine-owners had forced into being a labour supply to serve the needs of their mines. But the mineworkers — and those who worked in the industries that grew up with the mines — refused to remain mere units in a labour supply.

In the years that followed, more organised resistance developed, both politically and at the place of work. Workers began to make their own history.

This is a story which must be told another time.

Footnotes

CHAPTER 2
1. De Kiewiet, *A History of South Africa, Social and Economic*, chapter 5.
2. C.V. Sutherland, *Gold*, page 165.

CHAPTER 4
1. Pratt, *The Real South Africa*, published 1912.

CHAPTER 5
1. Presidential address to the Annual General Meeting of the Chamber of Mines, March 1912 — quoted by F.A. Johnstone, *Class, Race and Gold*.
2. Transvaal Labour Commission Reports 1903.
3. Reported in the *SA Mining Journal*, 23 September 1893.

CHAPTER 6
1. Presidential address to the Annual General Meeting of the Chamber of Mines, March 1912.
2. *Native Life in South Africa* by Sol. T. Plaatje, is to be published by Ravan Press in 1981.

CHAPTER 7
1. Presidential address to the Annual General Meeting of the Chamber of Mines, March 1912.
2. Cape Hansard 1894, page 362 — quoted by Van der Horst, *Native Labour in SA*.
3. Presidential address to the Annual General Meeting of the Chamber of Mines, March 1912.
4. Quoted by C. Bundy, *The Emergence and Decline of a South African Peasantry*. (This paper appears in *Contemporary South African Studies*, ed. Kallaway and Adler.)
5. Report of the Native Economic Commission, 1932.
6. From *Another Blanket*, Agency of Industrial Mission, page 25.
7. From *A Hundred Zulu Lyrics*, by Hugh Tracey.
8. 'The Sound of Africa Series,' Hugh Tracey — Record No AMA TR-85.

CHAPTER 8
1. From *Chopi Musicians*, Hugh Tracey.
2. 10th Chamber of Mines Annual Report 1898, page 89. (Much of the material in this Chapter comes from Kent McNamara's paper, 'The Development of a Recruitment Infrastructure: Labour Migration Routes to the Witwatersrand Gold Mines and Compound Accommodation — 1889 to 1912' — Paper presented at Wits. History Workshop, 1978, published in *South African Labour Bulletin*, Vol 4, no 3).
3. 6th Chamber of Mines Annual Report, 1894, page 35 — quoted by McNamara.
4. From a report to the Secretary for Native Affairs, 1906 — quoted in unpublished honours thesis by Sean Moroney, 'Industrial Conflict in a Labour Repressive Economy: Black Labour on the Transvaal Gold Mines 1901 — 1912'.
5. I am indebted to Moses Molepo of the African Studies Institute for this information.
6. Secretary for Native Affairs, 1903 — quoted by Moroney, unpublished thesis.
7. 10th Chamber of Mines Annual Report, 1898, page 4 — quoted by McNamara.
8. 6th Chamber of Mines Annual Report 1894, page 19.
9. From *Chopi Musicians* by Hugh Tracey.
10. Native Labour Commissioner's report, 6th Chamber of Mines Annual Report, 1894, page 69. — quoted by MacNamara, *SA Labour Bulletin*, Vol 4, no 3.
11. WNLA agents, Dr Samson's report to the Secretary for Native affairs, 1903 — quoted by Moroney.
12. Evidence to Mining Industry Board, 1922 — quoted by F.A. Johnstone in *Class, Race and Gold*.

CHAPTER 9
1. The Master and Servants Act was repealed in 1974. It has been suggested that an important reason for dropping this Act is that it has been replaced by a number of laws controlling labour — such as the Bantu Laws Amendment Act (67 of 1964), with the efficient application of influx control and the registration of black workers at labour bureaux. (Colin Bundy, 'The abolition of Master and Servants Act' — *SA Labour Bulletin*, May 1975.)
2. From the record Nyakynsa/Safwa (Wankie) — Hugh Tracey, 'The Sound of Africa Series'.

CHAPTER 10
1. Chamber of Mines Annual Report, January 1899 — quoted by B. Bozzoli in *The Political Nature of a Ruling Class*.
2. Conference between Transvaal Native Congress and the Minister of Justice, 7.4.1919 — quoted by Johnstone.
3. From *A Hundred Zulu Lyrics* — Hugh Tracey.
4. Evidence to the Industrial Commission of Enquiry, 1897 — quoted by Bozzoli.
5. Speech to Rand Mines Annual Meeting, 25.3.1903 — quoted by Bozzoli.
6. Quoted by P. Bonner, 'The Transvaal Native Congress 1917 — 1920: the Radicalisation of the Black Petty Bourgeoisie on the Rand'.
7. Quoted by Johnstone.
8. Quoted by Bozzoli.

CHAPTER 11:
1. I am indebted to Moroney (unpublished honours thesis) for many of the quotations in this chapter. For a summary of some of the themes in his thesis, see 'Mine Worker Protest on the Witwatersrand, 1901 — 1912' from *Essays in SA Labour History*, ed. E. Webster.
2. From Inspector's Report on the Compounds of the Rand fontein Group of Mines, October 1908 — quoted by Moroney.
3. Quoted by Johnstone.
4. From Dr Samson, District Health Officer's report to the Secretary for Native Affairs, 1903.
5. *Another Blanket*, page 5.
6. 'Randlords and Rotgut', by Charles van Onselen (published by Ravan Press), page 50. This paper deals fully with the mine-owners' use of liquor as a form of controlling their workers. 'Randlords and Rotgut' appears with a collection of van Onselen's essays on the early social history of working class life in South Africa in *Studies in the Social and Economic History of the Witwatersrand 1886 — 1914*, volumes I and II.
7. Native Grievances Inquiry Report 1914, para 474.
8. Secretary for Native Affairs Report from Acting Pass Commissioner, 1903 — quoted by Moroney, unpublished thesis.
9. Native Grievances Inquiry, 1914, para 33.
10. Quoted by A.P. Cartwright, *The Gold Mines*, page 220.
11. *Another Blanket*, page 23.
12. From *A Hundred Zulu Lyrics*, Hugh Tracey.
13. All quoted by Moroney, unpublished thesis.
14. These figures are taken from Moroney and from 'The Transvaal Labour Crisis, 1901 — 1906' by D. Denoon, published in the *Journal of African History*, vol 8, 1967
15. Quoted by Moroney.
16. Quoted by Moroney.
17. Native Grievances Inquiry Report, 1914, para 507.
18. This poem appeared in *Staffrider*, vol 2, no 3, July/August 1979.
19. From *A Hundred Zulu Lyrics* by Hugh Tracey. (This is a Xhosa song popular with Zulus.)
20. From *Chopi Musicians* by Hugh Tracey.
21. From the Rouge-Maputo district. Record AMA/TR-13 in the 'Sounds of Africa Series', Hugh Tracey.

CHAPTER 12
1. Quoted in *The Political Nature of a Ruling Class* by B. Bozzoli.
2. Quoted in *Class, Race and Gold* by F.A. Johnstone.
3. South African Native Affairs Commission 1903 — 1905; minutes of evidence — quoted by Bozzoli.
4. From a report to the Chamber of Mines Native Recruiting Corporation, 1925.
5. Evidence of mine-worker 'Tom' to the Native Grievances Inquiry, p 5, 28.10.1913 — quoted by Johnstone.
6. Evidence of mine-worker 'Kalaway' to Native Grievances Inquiry, p 19, 28.10.1913 — quoted by Johnstone.
7. From Van der Horst, *Native Labour in South Africa*, page 205 — 206.
8. From *Economics in South Africa*, N. Franklin.
9. Quoted by J.A. Hobson, *Imperialism*, 1902.
10. Quoted by J.A. Hobson, *Imperialism*, 1902.
11. Presidential address to Chamber of Mines Annual General Meeting.
12. From *The Boer War*, T. Pakenham.

13. G. Albu's evidence to Industrial Commission of Enquiry, reported in *SA Mining Journal*, 24.4.1897 — quoted by Bozzoli.

CHAPTER 14

1. President of the Chamber of Mines in a speech to a monthly meeting, September 1906 — quoted by Bozzoli.
2. For more information about Chinese workers on the Rand, see *Chinese Mine Labour in the Transvaal*, P. Richardson.
3. Quoted by Bozzoli.
4. From Moroney, unpublished thesis.

CHAPTER 15

1. From 'Supply and Control of Labour on the Rand, 1895 — 1924' — unpublished mimeo by E. Webster.
2. Transvaal Labour Importation Ordinance of 1904 — quoted by Johnstone, page 67.
3. Quoted in *Comrade Bill*, R.K. Cope.
4. From the Transvaal Mining Industry Commission 1904 — quoted by Van der Horst, *Native Labour in South Africa*.
5. From the Transvaal Indigency Commission, 1908 — quoted by Van der Horst.
6. From 'Supply and Control of Labour on the Rand 1895 — 1924', unpublished mimeo by E. Webster.
7. From *Comrade Bill*, R.K. Cope.
8. Figures from Van der Horst.
9. From 'Phthisis and the White Working Class on the Rand', E. Katz, unpubl. paper presented to 1978 Wits. History Workshop. See also 'The Migration of Miners' Pthisis between Cornwall and the Transvaal 1876 — 1918', Burke and Richardson, from *Labour, Townships and Protest*, ed Bozzoli.
10. From *Comrade Bill*, R.K. Cope.
11. From Government Commission Enquiry 1914 — quoted by Rob Davies, 'The Class Character of South Africa's Industrial Conciliation Legislation' from *Essays in Southern African Labour History*, ed E. Webster.
12. From *Comrade Bill*, R.K. Cope.
13. Increased production during those years was also assisted by technical improvements.

CHAPTER 16

1. Evidence to Mining Industry Commission by S. Reyerbach, Chairman of Rand Mines, 13.6.1907 — quoted by S. Moroney, 'Mine Worker Protest on the Witwatersrand: 1901 — 1912', from *Essays in Southern African Labour History*, ed. E. Webster.
2. Memorandum of Native Labour Supply, Pritchard, Director of Native Labour Bureau — quoted by Moroney, unpublished thesis.
3. Evidence by Buckle for Native Grievances Enquiry Report, par 310, page 42.
4. J.H. Johns, Consulting Engineer in evidence to the Mining Industry Commission 1907 — quoted by Moroney.
5. Report to Secretary for Native Affairs, 1902 — quoted by Moroney, unpublished thesis.
6. Secretary for Native Affairs Report 1907 — quoted by Moroney, unpublished thesis.
7. Reported in *SA Mining Journal*, 26.6.1896 — quoted by Bozzoli.
8. Evidence of the General Superintendent of the Native Recruiting Corporation to the Witwatersrand Disturbances Commission (1913) — quoted by Johnstone.
9. Sir George Albu, reported in the *SA Mining Review*, June 1907.
10. Report by Sub-Inspector, SAP, Benoni, to District Commandant, SAP, Boksburg, 4.2.1916 — quoted by Johnstone.
11. Reported by Native Constable R. Moorosi at a meeting on 29.6.1918.
12. Reported by Native Constable Arthur, Sergeant A.N. Turner and Sergeant J. Bland to Commissioner of Police, on the meeting of 19.6.1918 — quoted by Johnstone.
13. Report of the Commission of Inquiry into African Unrest on the Witwatersrand in 1918 — quoted by Johnstone.
14. Statement of the Transvaal Native Congress to the Low Grade Mines Commission 1919 — 1920 — quoted by Johnstone.
15. Minutes of a conference between Minister of Justice and Transvaal Native Congress, Pretoria, 7.4.1919 — quoted by Johnstone.
16. 18 October 1918, Reported by Native Constable Jali — quoted by Johnstone.
17. Report of Native Detective N. Sibisi to the Commissioner, SAP, on a meeting on 3 April 1919 — quoted by Johnstone.
18. Report of Detective J. King to Commanding Officer, SAP, Roodepoort, 6.3.1918 — quoted by Johnstone in the 'IWA on the Rand: Socialist Organising Among Black Workers on the Rand, 1917 — 1918', from *Labour Townships and Protest*, ed. Bozzoli.
19. Report of District Commandant, SAP, East Rand-Boksburg to Commissioner, SAP, 10.2.1920 — quoted by Johnstone in *Race, Class and Gold*'
20. Speech of the President of the Chamber of Mines, Annual General Meeting, March 1920 — quoted by Johnstone.
21. Spokesman for the workers of the Knights Deep Mine — quoted in *Comrade Bill*, page 215.
22. J. Fulford, District Commander, SAP Boksburg to Deputy Commissioner, Transvaal Division, 4.3.1920 — quoted by Johnstone.
23. Quoted by Johnstone, *Class, Race and Gold*.
24. Quoted by P. Bonner, 'The Transvaal Native Congress 1917 — 1920: The Radicalisation of the Black Petty Bourgeoisie on the Rand'.
25. P. Bonner, 'The Transvaal Native Congress 1917 — 1920: The Radicalisation of the Black Petty Bourgeoisie on the Rand'.
26. 'The South African Native National Congress' changed its name to the 'African National Congress' in 1925.
27. Quoted by E. Roux, *Time Longer than Rope*.
28. From *Comrade Bill*, R.C. Cope. Another translation of this leaflet is quoted by Johnstone, 'The IWA on the Rand', in *Labour, Townships and Protest*, ed. B. Bozzoli.

CHAPTER 17

1. Report of Native Detective M. Ngwenye to Commissioner of Police on a meeting dated 26.1.1919.
2. Evidence in 1921 Unemployment Commission — quoted by Johnstone.
3. Employer's evidence to Transvaal Indigency Commission 1908 — quoted by Johnstone.
4. Report and Minutes of Evidence of Select Committee of House of Assembly on European Employment and Labour Conditions, 1913 — quoted by Johnstone.
5. Letter from P. Tarbutt, Director of Goldfields Limited, Chairman of Village Main Reef Mine, to the Transvaal Labour Commission 1903 — quoted by Bozzoli.
6. Reported in *SA Mining Journal*, March 1897.
7. C. Hanau, President of Johannesburg Consolidated Investment Co. Limited, in a speech at the Annual Meeting, 1903 — quoted by Johnstone.
8. *SA Mining Journal*, editorial November 1892 — quoted by Bozzoli.
9. As above.
10. As above.
11. L. Reyersbach, Chairman's address to Annual General Meeting of the Rand Mines Limited, 23 March, 1904.
12. J.H. Johns in a speech to the Association of Mine Managers, 1894.
13. Evidence and minutes to the Wages and Economic Commission, 1925.
14. 'Origins of Class Formation in the Diamond Fields', D. Ginsberg — unpublished paper delivered at Seminars on Contemporary Labour, University of Natal.

CONCLUSION

1. Lionel Phillips' speech to the Chamber of Mines, 1893 — from *The Golden Transvaal*, published 1893.
2. George Albu, reported in *SA Mines*, 14.3.1903 — quoted by Bozzoli.
3. President of the Chamber of Mines to Annual General Meeting, March 1912 — quoted by Johnstone.
4. Editor, *SA Mining Journal*, 30.11.1895.
5. Quoted in *Man's Worldly Goods*, L. Huberman, Chap XVI.

Bibliography

Much of South African history has dealt with 'great men' and the ways in which they shaped our past.

In libraries you will also find dozens of beautifully-illustrated, expensive books on the industrial development of the Rand, its wealth and its 'colourful' early days.

But in all these collections of books, little is said of those who produced the wealth, the workers — especially black workers — and the part they played in history. Their full story is as yet unwritten.

Only in recent years have a significant number of South African historians started to ask questions about 'the people'. Who were they? Where did they come from? What happened to them? How did they shape their lives?

Slowly, a picture is emerging. In many ways it is a familiar picture, because it is very much part of people's daily lives; but it is only now being written by academic historians.

Some of these writings are so new that they have not yet been published. Some that have been published are banned. Those that remain, and which I have used for this book, I list below:

P. Abrahams, *Mine Boy.*

T. Adler ed., *Perspectives in Southern Africa.*

Agency of Industrial Mission, *Another Blanket.*

B. Bozzoli ed., *Labour, Townships and Protest.*

B. Bozzoli, *The Political Nature of a Ruling Class.*

C. Bundy, 'The Abolition of the Masters and Servants Act', *SA Labour Bulletin*, vol 2, no 1, May 1975.

R.K. Cope, *Comrade Bill.*

R. Davies, *Capital, State and White Labour in Southern Africa 1900 — 1960.*

B. Davidson, *Black Mother.*

B. Davidson, *Old Africa Rediscovered.*

C. de Kiewiet, *A History of South Africa, Social and Economic.*

D. Denoon, *Southern Africa Since 1800.*

D. Denoon, *The Grand Illusion.*

N. Franklin, *Economics in South Africa.*

L. Huberman, *Man's Worldly Goods.*

F.A. Johnstone, *Class, Race and Gold.*

E. Katz, *A Trade Union Aristocracy.*

P. Kallaway and T. Adler ed., *Contemporary South African Studies*, Volumes I and II (Research Papers, Wits. University).

M. Legassick, 'South Africa: Capital Accumulation and Violence', *Economy and Society*, Vol III, no 3, 1974.

J.K. McNamara, 'Migration Routes to the Gold Mines and Compound Accomodation', *SA Labour Bulletin*, Vol 4, no 3.

S.T. Plaatje, *Native Life in South Africa.*

T. Pakenham, *The Boer War.*

J. Pratt, *The Real South Africa.*

P. Richardson, *Chinese Mine Labour in the Transvaal.*

E. Roux, *Time Longer Than Rope.*

ed L. Thomson & M. Wilson, *Oxford History of South Africa.*

H. Tracy, *A Hundred Zulu Lyrics.*

H. Tracy, *Chopi Musicians.*

S. van der Horst, *Native Labour in South Africa.*

C. van Onselen, *Chibaro.*

C. van Onselen, *Studies in the Social & Economic History of the Witwatersrand 1886 — 1914, Vol I: New Babylon.*

P. Walshe, *The Rise of African Nationalism in South Africa; the African National Congress.*

E. Webster ed., *Essays in Southern African Labour History.*